TEACHING

Exploring New Frontiers for Learning

International Society for Technology in Education
PORTLAND, OREGON · ARLINGTON, VIRGINIA

MICHELLE ZIMMERMAN

Dedication

For the promise I made to them in 2007, I dedicate this book to the children who made my research possible because they spoke—and to those whose voices are yet to be heard.

Teaching AI

Exploring New Frontiers for Learning
Michelle Zimmerman

PROJECT EDITORS: Emily Reed and Valerie Witte
DEVELOPMENTAL EDITOR: Camille Cole
COPY EDITORS: Nicole Krueger and Stephanie Argy
PROOFREADER: Corinne Gould
INDEXER: Wendy Allex
BOOK DESIGN AND PRODUCTION: Danielle Foster
COVER DESIGN: Edwin Ouellette

Library of Congress Cataloging-in-Publication Data
Names: Zimmerman, Michelle Renee, author.
Title: Teaching AI : exploring new frontiers for learning / Michelle Zimmerman.
Description: Portland, Oregon : International Society for Technology in Education, [2018] | Includes bibliographical references and index. |
Identifiers: LCCN 2018033144 (print) | LCCN 2018047843 (ebook) | ISBN 9781564847270 (mobi) | ISBN 9781564847287 (epub) | ISBN 9781564847294 (pdf) | ISBN 9781564847058 (pbk.)
Subjects: LCSH: Artificial intelligence—Educational applications. | Artificial intelligence—Study and teaching. | Human-computer interaction—Study and teaching.
Classification: LCC LB1028.43 (ebook) | LCC LB1028.43 .Z56 2018 (print) | DDC 371.33/4—dc23
LC record available at https://lccn.loc.gov/2018033144
First Edition
ISBN: 978-1-56484-705-8
Ebook version available.

Printed in the United States of America
ISTE® is a registered trademark of the International Society for Technology in Education.

About ISTE

The International Society for Technology in Education (ISTE) is a nonprofit organization that works with the global education community to accelerate the use of technology to solve tough problems and inspire innovation. Our worldwide network believes in the potential technology holds to transform teaching and learning.

ISTE sets a bold vision for education transformation through the ISTE Standards, a framework for students, educators, administrators, coaches and computer science educators to rethink education and create innovative learning environments. ISTE hosts the annual ISTE Conference & Expo, one of the world's most influential edtech events. The organization's professional learning offerings include online courses, professional networks, year-round academies, peer-reviewed journals and other publications. ISTE is also the leading publisher of books focused on technology in education. For more information or to become an ISTE member, visit iste.org. Subscribe to ISTE's YouTube channel and connect with ISTE on Twitter, Facebook and LinkedIn.

ABOUT THE AUTHOR

 **MICHELLE ZIMMERMAN** has worked in multiple areas of education, from apprenticeship and co-teaching to research, leadership, and educator training, and she has taught all ages from 3 through 16. She received her Ph.D. in Learning Sciences and Human Development from the University of Washington College of Education in Seattle, and her research on learning design has been recognized with multiple awards. At Renton Prep Christian School, she has put her research into practice with blended, authentic learning environments, in which students learn to become mentor teachers and researchers. Under her leadership, Renton Prep has been selected by Microsoft to be a Showcase School since 2015, and in September 2018, was selected as the first K–12 Microsoft Flagship School in the United States. Since 2007 she has done presentations around the world, including at the American Education Research Association, DigiPen, ISTE, New York Academy of Medicine, New York Academy of Sciences, NYU Polytechnic School of Engineering, UCLA CRESST, educational technology conferences, and multiple universities. Her students have been presenting and co-authoring with her since 2011. She has been invited to add perspective to global leadership events at the headquarters of Microsoft, Google, and T-Mobile.

PREFACE

In fall 2017, ISTE was awarded a multi-year grant from General Motors to support the development of new resources in the field of artificial intelligence (AI) in K-12 education. The general goal of this initiative is to create scalable, best-in-class professional learning experiences for educators who could spread the knowledge of a variety of approaches to using AI in classrooms. Another important goal is to engage educators working with underrepresented student populations who might otherwise not consider AI as relevant to them to explore interdisciplinary associated careers.

Our collaboration with GM addresses the mismatch between the skills needed in the workforce and those developed in basic and post-secondary education. Through our AI K-12 Explorations online course, we are working with more than 500 technology coordinators, instructional coaches, and computer science educators to prepare them to help classroom-based educators explore and integrate AI technologies in ways that cultivate student-driven explorations and practical use in school environments.

The ISTE book *Teaching AI: Exploring New Frontiers for Learning* examines what AI is, how it works, and how educators can use it to better prepare students in a world with increasing human-computer interaction. It is our goal that this book will help educators engage students in project-based learning with a focus on exploring the aspects of AI technology with the potential to solve real problems in society and its interdisciplinary applicability to different aspects of our lives.

ISTE AI work would not have been possible without the grant support of GM Corporate Giving and Hina Baloch, Manager of Global Social Impact and STEM Education.

v

ACKNOWLEDGMENTS

"Do you hear what these children are saying?"

"Yes," he answered.

(Matthew 21:16)

I want to acknowledge my role models, because they have influenced my decision to accept the challenge of writing this book.

Artificial intelligence is a controversial topic, and one that rarely includes underrepresented voices. It is time to bring young people into the conversations on challenging topics that will directly impact their lives in the future. My greatest role models have taken the time to listen to children and to care about what they have to say, demonstrating that children have value as people.

My grandmother, Florence Merz, listened to the voices of young people that others had disregarded. She dedicated her short life to bringing equity and social justice to children, and I heard the stories of what it was like for her to be ahead of her time. In our new frontier with AI, we need people like her to reduce bias and increase equity.

My mother, Gloria Zimmerman, has followed in her mother's footsteps, working in special education and with special needs populations. She models strength and delivers life-changing positive impact by truly listening, even when words aren't audible. She has mastered reaching young people who are at risk of giving up on life because they have undergone severe trauma, or because they ask questions that no one has dared to ask before and that aren't well received by others. She listens, finds their greatest strengths, and helps them soar.

When my own challenges seemed insurmountable, she asked me a simple, profound question that allowed me to persist in speaking, writing, and helping transform education: "If what you do can positively impact the life of one child, is it worth it?" A small victory can change the course of one life and impact many others in a future beyond what we can imagine.

Had it not been for my father, David-Paul Zimmerman, I would not have challenged myself to keep learning the latest technology. In graduate school, he was the first in his program to type his thesis on a Commodore 64, printing it out with a dot-matrix printer. In the 1980s, he realized that education needed to use the latest technology, and he brought a computer into our home. In 2008, he made the decision to transform the school my grandmother had founded, reinventing it to help young people engage with the latest technology and prepare for the future. He introduced me to ISTE in 2010, signing me up for the conference in Denver, then telling me where I was going and why. He brought me into a new frontier for learning.

Daniel Boirum encouraged me to persist in helping young people engage with controversial topics through education. In 2009, when I was first implementing 1:1 laptops, multiple perspectives, and primary sources into my classroom, he wrote me a letter that changed the way I approached teaching. He told me I would know I was successful as an educator when my students realized there was no easy answer—and didn't even know how to give an answer. His framing reminded me that there are gray areas in humanity. We can avoid those to simplify learning, or we can help young people navigate them to understand complexity while developing compassion. Daniel changed the way I taught with technology. His words from a decade ago strongly influenced the design of this book, as did his ongoing feedback and willingness to provide blunt critiques. Without him, and his young son's philosophical question, "Is it a good robot or a bad robot?", the concept of the introductions for each chapter would not have existed.

Adrian Murias planted a seed and showed me that the beauty of language and human emotion cannot be replicated by any machine. He inspired Chapter 3 through his discussions on language, identity, culture, family history, DNA, and genetics. His story of a teacher who loved science as much as he did, and who encouraged him to keep asking questions, showed me the impact an educator can have on the life of a student. Adrian is now an inventor with multiple patents who is revolutionizing truck and engine design. Our collaboration began in 2013, and then in 2016 when I developed a dream of working on a project that would involve both the future of education and General Motors, he encouraged me to make it a reality. He was there for me during cyberattacks and other manifestations of the dark side of technology, and he and showed me again the importance of human connection when technology is used in destructive ways. Without him, the chapter on ethics would not have been the same.

I'm indebted to my brother Matthew Zimmerman for helping me learn how science fiction can address deep aspects of the human condition. He has also seen things in me before I saw them in myself, and he launched my collaboration with Valve and my four years of research on gaming with Portal 2 in the classroom. With the questions he posed and the details he brought to my attention, he shifted the direction of this book. The concepts of implicit learning and transfer of learning would not have become clear had he not pointed me that way.

At a time when there is increased interest in women role models for girls in STEM fields, I want to acknowledge the importance of men who can also profoundly impact women in STEM and in leadership. Roger Soder, Jonathan Grudin, Ashok Goel, Jason Osborne, Fabio Coronel, and Ira Sockowitz have provided perspective, re-shaped my thinking, and supported the productive struggle inherent in exploring new frontiers for learning. Without each of them, this book wouldn't exist as it is now.

Learning is a sociocultural process. One person alone cannot juggle all the information and data necessary to adapt learning effectively for an entire classroom of learners who are very different from each other. AI holds promise to augment and support the crucial work of educators, rather than replacing them. Knowing who we are as people and what we want to be as a society in the future are crucial to defining the goals we set to educate our future generations, and how we meet those goals together.

CONTENTS

Contents

CHAPTER 2

Preparing Students for the Future   21

CHAPTER 3

Approaches to Teaching with AI   47

CHAPTER 4

How AI Can Support Student Learning   87

CHAPTER 5
How AI Can Support Teachers

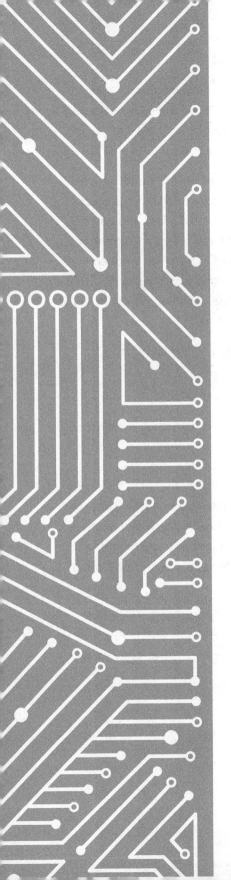

INTRODUCTION

If you have picked up this book, it means you are invested in preparing young people for a future that includes artificial intelligence (AI).

There is no single definition that encapsulates all AI. Much of the information about it appears contradictory. You may hear people who have been researching AI for decades say that AI does not exist yet, but that components necessary for it to work do exist and are becoming more sophisticated. You may see discussions in the media that use the term AI to refer to applications, robots, or systems, and you might wonder whether AI does actually exist. In all the confusion, it can be difficult to figure out what, exactly, counts as AI.

Part of the challenge is that the definition continues to shift as technologies become more advanced and normalized. For example, some people previously considered calculators evidence of AI, but we now see calculators as a basic piece of technology and do not assume they are replicating human intelligence. It can be argued that advances in technology raise the bar for AI, which makes it more difficult to pin down what counts as AI.

Some people define the primary goal of AI as replicating human intelligence. Others suggest AI should augment human intelligence but not be able to replace or replicate it. Those different perspectives on the technology's goals can also shift the way people define AI and how they decide which technologies it encompasses.

Part of the difficulty in agreeing upon a definition is that people are still debating what counts as human intelligence—not just in computer science, but also in biological sciences and psychology. Is it an IQ test score? Is it the ability to transfer learning and apply it? Is it the capacity to interact socially? Is it the ability to calculate complex algorithms? Are there multiple types of intelligence or not? If it is that hard to agree on what counts as human intelligence, then it is reasonable to assume that variances in what machines are capable of would also make it difficult to arrive at a single definition. To illustrate the problem, *Merriam-Webster* (2018) defines artificial intelligence as:

1. a branch of computer science dealing with the simulation of intelligent behavior in computers

2. the capability of a machine to imitate intelligent human behavior

By this definition, one could argue that a machine capable of constructing a haiku poem based on a photograph of nature imitates intelligent human behavior. However, its lack of emotion, culture, and awareness of tradition means it is not a true replica of human intelligence. Similarly, a machine that can win chess but cannot beat a human at a less sophisticated game like tic-tac-toe does not really simulate intelligent behavior because it cannot transfer its learning strategy from one game to another. Autocorrect might also appear to be an imitation of intelligent behavior—until it replaces what we meant to say with something no human would ever think was appropriate. Is that truly a replication of human intelligence?

Techopedia (2018) defines artificial intelligence as "an area of computer science that emphasizes the creation of intelligent machines that work and react like humans." It also lists some of the activities that computers with artificial intelligence are designed for, such as:

- Speech recognition
- Learning
- Planning
- Problem solving

In writing this book, I sought out experts in the AI field and asked them to weigh in on the confusion that educators may encounter when researching AI on their own. These authorities have a depth of understanding supported by years of experience and work invested in the subject.

Ashok Goel is a professor of computer science and cognitive science at Georgia Institute of Technology's School of Interactive Computing. His role as director of the school's PhD program in human-centered computing enables him to see AI from the perspective of the information world. As coordinator of the faculty consortium on Creativity, Learning & Cognition and co-coordinator of the faculty consortium on Interactive Intelligence, he offers insight into how AI interacts with the human world. His work as director of the school's Design & Intelligence Laboratory and co-director of Georgia Tech's Center for Biologically Inspired Design influences how he sees AI's impact in the physical world. People who define AI by focusing on one particular domain or subsection of a field may not consider another area as essential to the definition. But when we consider multiple domains, from biology to computer science to creativity and cognition, we gain a broader perspective that helps us to see the way these definitions intersect. Goel's well-rounded range of professional experiences gives him that perspective, as well as the ability to offer clarity on what can be a confusing new frontier for educators.

In personal communication with Goel (May 22, 2018), he confirmed that general artificial intelligence does not yet exist. No one has yet created a machine that replicates human intelligence by combining the abilities to interact, reason, process, respond, and be creative with emotion like a human.

Goel shared a visual diagram he created to help others understand how AI's various pieces fit together. Imagine a large circle, which represents all of AI. Within that circle, narrow applications of AI already exist. Facebook's ability to recognize faces in photos is just one example. The semantic web, which uses HTML and tags to translate sensory information into a language that machines understand, is another. Within the larger circle, these pieces of AI are illustrated by three smaller circles that overlap like a Venn diagram (Figure I.1).

Figure I.1
Venn diagram illustrating aspects of AI and how they correspond to the real world (Goel & Davies, 2019).

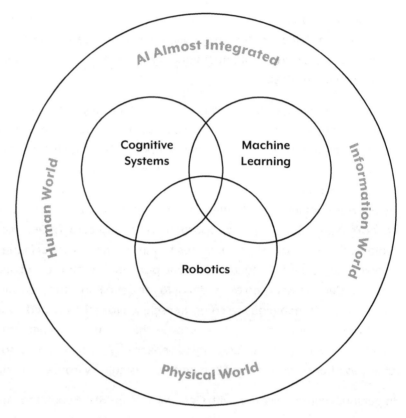

Each of those smaller circles represents a known aspect necessary to solve the challenge of creating general AI: cognitive systems, machine learning, and robotics. These three aspects of AI are not strictly delineated. Some technologies fit into more than one category, in which case they would fall within the overlapped areas of the Venn diagram.

COGNITIVE SYSTEMS deal with the human world. They include chatbots as well as cognitive computing systems like IBM Watson, which has been used in applications ranging from health care to trivia games to helping young children learn vocabulary.

ROBOTICS deal with the physical world and can move around and interact with humans. One example is the glove that General Motors and NASA developed to help reduce the impact of repetitive tasks on the human body (Vanian, 2016).

MACHINE LEARNING deals with the information world. It refers to machines that not only process vast amounts of data, but that have the capacity to get better and better at it.

Based on current knowledge, AI can work if all three systems are integrated and know how to communicate with and learn from each other in meaningful ways. Goel says some people joke that AI should stand for "almost integrated," because no one has figured out how to integrate robotics, cognitive systems, and machine learning to create general AI. He also believes his diagram may be missing some circles for yet-undiscovered elements necessary for true artificial general intelligence.

If we focus too closely on merely integrating the existing components of AI, we risk missing important pieces such as cognitive sciences, human development, and sociocultural perspectives. Paul Allen asserted that discovering the unknowns in neuroscience will help solve the challenge of creating AI (2011), but Goel pointed out the limitations of a neuroscience perspective focused solely on understanding how the human brain works. Humans are not just a body and a brain working in isolation. We learn gradually, in context—and as we will see in the second chapter, much of our learning happens in the presence of others. According to developmental molecular biologist John Medina, our experiences influence how our brains are wired (2008). No two human brains are exactly alike, partly because of our unique experiences.

Defining the various elements of AI can also be tricky. For example, at what point is a machine considered a robot? For the purposes of this book, we will use the definition proposed by Crash Course, a series of PBS educational videos for learners of all ages, which describes robots as "machines capable of carrying out a series of actions automatically guided by computer control." Watch the two Crash Course videos in the Understanding AI section to compare the difference between robots and AI.

UNDERSTANDING AI

Watch the Crash Course video on AI and machine learning to understand the heart of machine learning, which sits inside the more ambitious goal of artificial intelligence. From spam filters and self-driving cars to cutting-edge medical diagnosis and real-time language translation, watch how computers learn from data and apply that knowledge to make predictions and decisions: **tinyurl.com/y9uojrug**

Watch the Crash Course video on robotics: **tinyurl.com/y9sw82sg**

Who Is This Book For?

This book offers perspectives on how people in education and other fields are understanding, using, and training with AI, which is already shifting the landscape of human-computer interactions. This may be your introduction to AI, or you may have been studying, researching, or developing AI for a while.

IF YOU ARE NEW TO AI

If you are new to AI and are passionate about education, this book can help you understand what it is, how it currently exists in technologies you or your students may already be using, and how to help prepare your students for a future in which AI will play an even bigger role in their lives and careers. This is not just about coding or finding a website that can teach your students to create AI for themselves. As we prepare students for a future in which today's jobs may be replaced by machines such as electronic kiosks, assembly lines, chatbots, and neural-networks, we need to be aware of the many socio-cultural implications surrounding AI.

Our students need to understand who they are as people; why societies, cultures, and traditions are important; how to treat others with respect; and how to become stronger in areas where machines do not excel, while learning about machines' ability to augment our own human capacity. Students will need to know how to learn, unlearn, and relearn to remain relevant in a constantly shifting job market. Training in design thinking, STEM (science, technology, engineering, and math), and project-based learning can assist with developing this mindset.

Students also need to know how to examine and intentionally seek out multiple perspectives to minimize bias that could be detrimental when amplified by the power of machine learning. For that reason, this book intentionally highlights voices and perspectives of people from around the world in different career fields and life stages. The diverse locations and backgrounds of these individuals serve as a reminder that diversity matters. We need to be diligent in seeking out multiple perspectives, and model that for our learners.

Living in a world with AI will require students to become not only continual learners, but also teachers—first to other humans, then to computers, as they train and interact with machines. Young people who wish to develop AI in the future must be capable of considering a range of implications, including legal protection, ethical considerations, and what will happen when machines become more like humans. Will we treat AI as machines or as humans? These are critical conversations as we attempt to impose order on the Wild West frontier of AI.

Future careers will become increasingly interdisciplinary as students work with the various components that are part of AI, like robotics, cognitive systems, and machine learning. As educators, we have the opportunity to model our openness to learning and teaching more than one subject domain. While machines are often specific to a particular domain, humans have the ability to cross domains and create applications across fields. That is why this book makes unexpected connections between the arts, sciences, linguistics, ethics, and other areas. You will see examples of careers and hands-on applications that show the cross-disciplinary nature of AI. For example, Pixar Animation Studios merges storytelling, art, computer science, and mathematics to create animated films. Your students can use free tools to practice this interdisciplinarity.

This book can serve as a guide to help educators see a broader picture of learning in which a sociocultural perspective helps our learners toward success in a future with AI. It is not just about computer science or STEM. This book tells the story of AI through diverse human perspectives, and it challenges you to make your own connections. The stories related here are meant not only to challenge your perspective as a reader, but also to be used in discussions with learners. They are intended to demonstrate something only humans can do: make connections across seemingly unrelated domains. We know literature, linguistics, philosophy, and the arts help foster this type of thinking while building empathy. A machine can process large amounts of data much faster than a human, but we can remain relevant by strengthening our ability to transfer learning from one context to another; to make connections across domains to identify innovative solutions; and to abstract ideas and create something that conveys emotion, culture, tradition, and purposeful solutions.

IF YOU ARE EXPERIENCED WITH AI

If you are currently working with AI and are passionate about education, this book can help spark ideas or create connections in ways that may assist you as you continue to push the boundaries of artificial intelligence. It can also help you become more aware of the challenges educators experience in the classroom. As the design thinking methodology points out, design needs to begin with empathy. Empathy can lead to asking questions about how to solve challenges that may be relevant to others, but not necessarily to yourself. It can also lead to seeking multiple perspectives.

Why Should You Read this Book?

A better understanding of AI can help you make informed decisions that will impact the future of your learners. AI may seem like a relatively new and possibly overwhelming concept, or one that is only of interest to advanced coders. But AI is relevant to everyone, regardless of their interest in coding.

For many of us, our awareness of AI has developed through popular culture. Movies, for example, help visualize and articulate the contents of our imagination, often leaving viewers curious about what a world with AI will be like. These films often conflate robotics with AI, as in *Ex Machina* (Garland, 2015) and *Big Hero 6* (Hall & Williams, 2014). The first takes a cautionary, dystopian tone, while the second imagines what might be possible when AI is able to support human healing through continued legacy and augmented medical assistance.

Artificial intelligence is not just science fiction. It is already being used to enable people to perform their work better, with more speed and accuracy. Dr. Iain Hennessey, the clinical leader for innovation at Alder Hey Children's Hospital in England, is harnessing the power of IBM Watson (IBM Corporation, 2017) to develop a chatbot that enables children at the hospital to interact with their parents, document their feelings, and ask questions while gaining immediate feedback. The use of the chatbot also provides valuable data to healthcare professionals to inform their future practice. Although very different than Baymax, the lovable robot that tries to solve medical needs in *Big Hero 6*, chatbots like this act as springboards to further medical innovations powered by AI. As chatbots collect data and respond to typical questions, doctors can have more time to focus on pressing issues and deliver more personalized service to patients.

Not all AI is as visible as Hennessey's chatbot, however. People across the globe are using AI to perform basic tasks, often without even realizing it. AI helps power many of the tools we use daily, including:

- Virtual personal assistants like Siri and Alexa
- Video games
- Self-driving cars (McFarland, 2015)
- Purchase prediction features for companies such as Target and Amazon
- Fraud detection used by banks to protect against credit card fraud

- Online customer support
- News generation for simple sports statistics and financial reports (Finley, 2015)
- Security surveillance
- Music and movie recommendation services such as Spotify and Netflix
- Smart home devices (Albright, 2016)

What does all this mean for students? The goal of this book is to help educators determine how to incorporate AI into their classrooms and determine what students need to know about living in a world with AI. We'll explore some of the various ways AI can augment education, including:

1. Educating learners about AI
2. Teaching learners to live in a world where they will be surrounded by AI
3. Helping educators understand how they can use AI to augment human ability

THE PERSPECTIVES

This book draws on a broad variety of expert voices to represent the field of AI. Readers will be exposed to global perspectives from a range of countries including highlights from work in Australia, Japan, and South Africa; voices from educators in other countries; and underrepresented student voices. Microsoft researcher Dr. Ece Kamar discusses the importance of understanding the domain you are working with as a developer and researcher working with AI (Huizinga, 2018). Graduate student Nile Wilson points out the importance of including clients, family caregivers, and medical professionals in the process of developing accessibility solutions for brain-computer interfaces that utilize AI (personal communication, May 2, 2018). In cross-disciplinary collaborations such as these, empathy in the design thinking process is an important component of finding effective solutions to people's problems. The same is true for education.

THE APPROACH

Some people prefer an analytical approach to investigating and applying AI. Others are engaged in imagining the emotional impact of human-computer interaction. For the latter, storytelling may make the most sense as a way to envision how AI will impact learners now and in the future. AI researcher Roger Schank (2018) argues that storytelling is our primary tool for making sense of the world and sharing useful information. For those who prefer an analytical approach or have not had much experience in the class-room, the chapter opening scenes, case studies, and student voices in this book will add another level of perspective on advancing education with AI. This may, in turn, assist in a development cycle with the end-user in mind or provoke developers to consider new questions in the design process.

ISTE STANDARDS FOR STUDENTS

Throughout this book, you will see the ISTE Standards for Students referenced in a variety of ways. Sometimes the connection between AI and the ISTE Standards will be explicit and obvious; other times it might emerge through a series of reflective questions. You can find the full ISTE Standards for Students in the appendix.

EQUITABLE AND ETHICAL

At this point, you may have questions about the logistics of teaching AI in your school. As one educator at a 2018 conference in Austin, Texas, asked:

> *"I see the value in learning about AI, but what can I do to convince and prepare administration, parents, and students in a school that does not even have technology yet?"*

Technology is just one component of preparing learners for a world with AI. They will also need to be able to grapple with the philosophical questions and logical argumen-tation that arise around AI (Vander Ark, 2017). They will need to develop their uniquely human abilities to perform the tasks AI cannot, such as finding connections between seemingly disconnected subjects and domains. Students can learn these skills with or without technology. Experts working with AI have become increasingly aware of the importance of cross-disciplinary collaboration as they develop AI systems. In this book, you will find interdisciplinary topics connecting design thinking, STEM, and ethics—all of which are crucial to ensure well-rounded interactions with AI.

To create an equitable world with AI, we remain vigilant in addressing concerns of bias, articulating goals for our society, and considering how education can help us achieve those goals. We can do this by starting with content that is usable in all settings, with or without access to technology, such as training young people to think, reason, respond, create, and fail. It is possible to help young people develop flexibility of thought and become empowered learners, knowledge constructors, innovative designers, creative communicators, and computational thinkers even without access to technology in the classroom.

Once learners are prepared with this mindset and begin interacting with technology inside or outside of school, you can help students use those skills to become successful digital citizens and global collaborators. AI can assist in all of this. As students master these skills in various ways, they will become better equipped to engage with and develop AI in the future. Educators can begin developing this mindset, discussing the ethical considerations of AI (Green, 2016), and helping students understand what it means to create and enforce new policies and regulations that may not exist yet—all without full access to technology in schools. In this way, educators can begin helping students, parents, faculty, and leadership to consider the dynamics and skills that will help build a solid foundation for AI in education.

What You Can Expect to Find in This Book

The first chapter explores what AI is through a brief history and discussion of the various components that make up AI. This will set the context for an introduction to examples of how educators are already using AI with the help of technologies and organizations such as IBM Watson, Adobe, and Sesame Workshop.

The second chapter focuses on why we should care about preparing students for a future with AI. The ISTE Standards for Students are not just another list of standards to check off—they help educators anchor their end goals for students to learning practices such as creating, redesigning, failing, and problem-solving. Aiming for these standards will create a solid foundation for student engagement with AI.

The third chapter presents approaches to teaching AI. These approaches include project-based learning, design thinking, systems thinking, AI in the classroom, and additional project resources and lesson plans. Questions and thoughts on this topic from educators around the world are also included in this chapter.

The fourth chapter dives into how AI can support student learning. Working with AI demands a multidisciplinary approach, and the integrated nature of STEM offers an authentic path for developing this approach. We'll also discover how adding the arts in STEM can inform our understanding of AI.

The fifth chapter discusses how AI can support educators by automating tasks and freeing up teacher time. We'll examine how one university professor is automating tasks for his 500 students by creating dynamic assessments that go beyond multiple choice and developing a chatbot that has changed how mechanical engineering students learn.

The sixth chapter delves into ethical issues and concerns. AI has the potential to create enormous positive change, but it also has the potential to incite fear. As educators, it is our responsibility to help direct controversial technologies for beneficial use and to train a new generation to use those technologies in a way that leaves the world—and humanity—better off. The reality is that any technology (or human characteristic) carries the potential for either positive impact or destruction and harm. With AI, we must consider ethical issues such as the loss of control and privacy, shifts in the job market due to automation, and legal implications.

The conclusion pulls all of these ideas together and provides a call to action for educators, while offering some concrete next steps for teaching and learning with AI.

Throughout this book, you may encounter vocabulary that is new to you. The glossary is there to assist educators in developing a common language for discussing AI. You will also find suggested activities and questions within each chapter to help you deepen your understanding, try out new concepts, and reflect on the information presented. The links provided will lead you to media artifacts that can help make your learning experience more dynamic while also providing additional resources you can use in your classroom with students, parents, and other educators. These resources come from a variety of trusted educational sources, including PBS LearningMedia, Sesame Workshop, Ted-Ed, Microsoft, Adobe, and Google, among others. You will also find references to films and other media you can use in class to start discussions on AI or inspire design thinking and STEM projects.

As you continue your journey with AI in education, consider the five- and six-year-olds of today, many of whom will be finishing their secondary education in the year 2030 (Holzapfel, 2018). As children learn, their brains take in large amounts of sensory information. They process that information, take some sort of action, and learn from the reaction. They may then adjust their approach or seek new information. As we explore the intersection between AI and humans, we can start asking more questions about not only our goals for young people as they complete formal education, but also our goals for AI in general (**tinyurl.com/y9xxjckv**). We can decide whether to focus our efforts on augmenting versus replicating human intelligence. In a 2018 Microsoft Research podcast titled Life at the Intersection of AI and Society (**tinyurl.com/y9xxjckv**), Dr. Ece, Kamar quotes her PhD advisor Barbara Grosz, who said, "We already know how to replicate human intelligence: we have babies. So, let's look for what can augment human intelligence, what can make human intelligence better."

Our young people will continue to be flooded with information, influencing their perspectives and opinions on humanity, jobs, politics, government, and nature. When it comes to AI and data mining, students will need to know the right questions to ask and how to search for information. They will need to be aware that for AI to work, data is being collected all the time from their voices, their faces, their keystrokes, their location on Google Maps, and the websites they engage with. They will need to understand more about privacy and who owns their data more than any generation that came before them—and they will need to know it at a much younger age. They will need to be able to solve new problems with unknown solutions and no precedents to draw upon. They will also need to learn how to not feel defeated if they do not arrive at a solution right away. All of these scenarios require asking many questions and engaging in many of discussions. When failure does occur, we can guide them to practice asking effective questions that will help them identify new goals, redesigns, or determine novel approaches, rather than repeating the same actions or behavior and expecting different results.

Kamar's research looks at two main aspects of AI: how to build systems that provide value for humans in daily tasks, and how humans can complement these AI systems. It is interesting to think about these two broad research categories as we begin our story of AI with a five-year-old boy, a six-year-old girl, and a robot.

CHAPTER 1
What Is AI?

Questioning Human-Computer Interaction

DRAMATIS PERSONAE

LEILA: Six-year-old girl

CUB: Five-year-old boy

SCENE

Leila and Cub are visiting a middle school learning space with their parents and younger brother.

TIME: April 2018

ACT 1

Scene 1

SETTING: School is not in session. The building is silent, absent the bustle, laughter, and exclamations of students. In an alcove marked by an orange and blue striped area rug, a scattering of lime green chairs and pillows invites visitors into a space designated for collaboration, quiet reading, media creation, and general innovation. A robot, just over three feet tall, stands in the corner.

AT RISE: Leila and Cub enter the alcove and spot the robot.

Figure 1.1
The children stare at what might be eyes or goggles. No one blinks—not Leila, Cub, nor the two plastic discs staring blankly from the robot.

LEILA: Why isn't it talking?

CUB: Is it a good robot or a bad robot?

The children inch toward the robot and proceed to inspect its wires, screws, arms, the wall plug, and the wheels that function as its feet. They want interaction. They want to know if it is friendly. Will it scare them, or will it shake hands with them? They are breathless.

As the two young people—almost the same height as the robot—wait for some sort of interaction, the robot remains lifeless. Made by middle school students, who programmed it to speak a few words and perform simple gestures, the robot does not have a mind of its own. It is not "intelligent." It is not receiving any sensory information. It is not analyzing Leila and Cub, nor is it processing vast amounts of data to read their reactions, find patterns, or adapt its behavior in an attempt to procure a different result.

The children, on the other hand, are taking in data as they study the robot in front of them. Cub attempts a friendly fist-bump in hopes of eliciting a reaction.

CUB: Why isn't it doing anything?

LEILA: Maybe it's out of batteries.

As they poke, prod, and even attempt voice commands, there seems to be a slight movement and sound from the robot. Leila jumps back and curls up under a nearby chair. She covers her face, then peeks out again.

While still uncertain whether the robot poses a threat, the youngsters remain fascinated. They approach it once more to re-examine its combination of screws and plastic wires. Why does it look like a person that should come to life? They continue their attempts to engage it, but the robot fails to react. They search for a reason why.

LEILA: It's a screw! It's missing a screw! I can fix this!

The two children begin a thorough investigation, searching the area for missing screws. They're not yet aware of a more likely explanation: the robot simply has not been programmed by humans to function the way the young people hope it will.

UNDERSTANDING AI ·

Leila and Cub hypothesized that getting the robot to interact with them might be as simple as finding a loose or missing screw. Leila believed if she just found that missing piece, the robot would respond as if it were human. Throughout the history of AI, people working to solve its grand problems have been looking for the loose screw—the key to replicating human intelligence in a machine. Even once they find it, they realize the challenge is more complex than originally anticipated (Brooks, 2018). To date, human cognition and intelligence remain superior to the capabilities of a computer (Allen, 2011). No machine has successfully passed the Turing Test by fooling people into believing it is human.

When their search fails to produce results, Leila and Cub start listing robots from popular culture, categorizing which are "good" and which are "bad." The examples they draw upon, from Wall-E and Eva to C-3PO and R2-D2, all depict robots that display human-like intelligence and emotion—or at least evoke an emotional response from us. By exploring what they already know about AI, the children are looking for patterns that might help them predict the robot's behavior.

End Scene 1

REFLECTING ON AI ·

- What were Leila and Cub expecting from this robot?
- What caused them frustration, and what did they do to mitigate their frustration?
- What prior knowledge did they have, and how did they apply it?
- What are some common perceptions about AI we get from media and films, and how might this have influenced the children's behavior and confusion?
- If young children like Leila and Cub are now expecting to see intelligent inter-action with a plastic robot that was only programmed to do very simple tasks, what will they expect to see as high school students?
- Will they have the same fears previous generations had about interacting with machines, or do those come with age, cultural influences (Nasir, Rosebery, Warren, & Lee, 2006), and biases indoctrinated by fears evoked from science fiction or cautionary dystopian storytelling?

What AI Is—and Isn't

In the scene above, Leila and Cub expected the robot to interact with them in an intelligent way—the way popular culture and science fiction have shown us robots should respond to humans. But they were interacting with a robot, not AI.

It's a common misconception that AI and robotics are the same. This may stem from science-fiction films that often depict AI housed within the form of a robot, or a body that appears human but is built out of wires and materials different from flesh and bone. Although the development of AI and robotics may go hand-in-hand—Rodney Brooks suggests in his paper "Intelligence without Reason" (1991) that work in mobile robotics has helped advance approaches to AI—they are two different technologies. While it is common to confuse a robot's capabilities with AI, such false impressions can lead to confusion, fear, or warnings of robots becoming intelligent enough to take our jobs and replace human interactions with robotic ones.

What many people don't realize is that not all robots are driven by AI—and while AI can be placed within the shell of a robot, it can also exist in a form that doesn't resemble any living creature at all. According to Microsoft's First Steps into Artificial Intelligence course (**tiny.cc/a3y7vy**), AI is a broad umbrella term for a type of tool that helps people work better and do more (J. Zimmerman, personal communication, May 9, 2018). There's a good chance you have experienced or used AI more than you realize. Personal assistants, chatbots, language translators, video games, smart cars, and facial recognition are all examples of AI. Purchase prediction by retailers like Target and Amazon, fraud detection in banks, online customer support, news generation for simple sports statistics and financial reports, security surveillance, music and movie recommendation services like Spotify and Netflix, and smart home devices all use AI (Albright, 2016).

This chapter and the next will explore the various technologies that fall under the umbrella term of AI, as well as the components that are necessary for AI to work—such as **machine learning**, **perception** and **machine problem-solving**.

PERSONAL ASSISTANTS

Personal Assistants, or personal digital assistants, such as Siri, Google Now, Cortana, and Alexa, can listen to your voice and respond to between 40% and 80% of questions asked. Some assistants are built-in features of mobile devices, laptops, or smart speakers.

As these applications improve, their capabilities and usage are expanding rapidly, with new products entering the market on a regular basis. An online poll in May 2017 found the most widely used personal assistants in the U.S. included Apple's Siri (34%), Google Assistant (19%), Amazon Alexa (6%), and Microsoft Cortana (4%) (Graham, 2017). Apple and Google have amassed significant user bases on smartphones, as has Microsoft on Windows personal computers, smartphones, and smart speakers. Amazon Alexa also has a substantial user base for smart speakers.

Personal assistants have the potential to significantly impact which skills students need to learn in school. As these tools become capable of taking on more tasks, some of the skills students are learning today will become obsolete. Coding is one example.

Wolfram|Alpha, the computational knowledge engine that runs Siri, aims to make all systematic knowledge immediately computable and accessible to everyone (**m.wolframalpha.com**). To that end, the company has developed a programming language that leverages AI to automatically generate low-level code, allowing programmers to operate at a higher level. According to founder Stephen Wolfram:

> One of our great goals with the Wolfram Language is to automate the process of coding as much as possible so people can concentrate on pure computational thinking. When one is using lower-level languages, like C++ and Java, there's no choice but to be involved with the detailed mechanics of coding. But with the Wolfram Language the exciting thing is that it's possible to teach pure high-level computational thinking, without being forced to deal with the low-level mechanics of coding. (**Wolfram, 2017**)

Students can experiment with this advanced programming language and practice their computational thinking skills using the Wolfram Programming Lab (**wolfram.com/programming-lab**).

While virtual assistant technology is developing quickly, it still has some limitations, such as failing to answer, mishearing questions, and a lack of support for languages other than English (Dellinger, 2018). Understandably, there is also some controversy regarding devices that are always listening, but that is the flip side of helping to build a repository of data from which machines can learn. There may also be ethical concerns regarding disclosure of whether users are talking to a bot or a real person. When Google recently offered a preview of its Google Assistant feature Duplex, the software's command of natural language "was so masterful that it was apparent the person on the other end had no idea he or she was talking to a machine" (Pachal, 2018).

CHATBOTS

Chatbots attempt to replicate human conversation though text chats, voice commands, or both. Machine learning, combined with a technology known as **natural language processing** (NLP), makes this an element of AI. Chatbots have the ability to mimic human conversation by recognizing the cadence in conversations, storing the patterns, and extracting them to imitate human behavior. This is one example of machine learning algorithms.

LANGUAGE TRANSLATORS

Most of us can speak faster than we type. Natural language processing allows the computer to translate what you speak into text, enabling **language translators** to do more than just translate from one language to another. Dictate (**dictate.ms**), a new project released through Microsoft Garage (**microsoft.com/en-us/garage**), is one example. There is also a language translator that will produce live subtitles, translated as you speak. The extension works with Outlook, Word, and PowerPoint for Windows, converting speech to text using the state-of-the-art speech recognition and AI imbued with Microsoft Cognitive Services, including the Bing Speech Application Programming Interface (API) and Microsoft Translator. Presentation Translator is a PowerPoint add-in that lets you add live subtitles to your presentation and translate the text in your PowerPoint document (Chansanchai, 2017). Microsoft's Language Translator project now offers both cloud and offline translations with language packs that support 44 languages, including Arabic, Simplified Chinese, French, German, Italian, Japanese, Korean, Portuguese, Russian, Spanish, and Thai (Tung, 2018).

Language translators can play a key role in helping students become global collaborators, allowing them to easily translate their content for an international audience. When a group of legislators from Japan visited our school last year, my students used natural language processing to demonstrate the intersection of tradition, culture, AI, and the creative process. They designed Japanense-inspired artwork using Sway, which is supported by machine learning, to document their creative process and translate their reflections for our international guests (**tinyurl.com/y8euo5dd**). The project allowed students to explore how AI can support traditional and cultural practices such as hand-generated art by enabling them to practice and draft concepts using no-mess digital ink.

FACIAL RECOGNITION

In addition to processing speech, technology is growing increasingly adept at recognizing faces. **Facial recognition** refers to a machine's ability to identify a person from a digital image. By comparing certain facial features to a database of images, the software can either pinpoint or verify a person's identity, making it useful for security systems as an alternative (or complement to) fingerprint or iris recognition.

Some researchers are concerned about the implications of facial recognition software. Questions about the future of policing have arisen with China's use of AI and facial recognition to fine jaywalkers via text (Grothaus, 2018). In the city of Shenzhen, which has been using software and cameras to project the faces of jaywalkers on a large screen near the intersection for everyone to see, police are now able to distribute tickets and fines to repeat offenders detected by AI. The software company is even partnering with social media platforms and local mobile phone carriers to text jaywalkers as soon as they cross the street.

Facial recognition also has implications for the classroom. One Chinese high school has begun employing the technology to monitor and analyze student behavior in the classroom (Chan, 2018). The software scans students' faces every 30 seconds, categorizing their facial expressions as well as actions such as reading, writing, or raising their hands. Meanwhile, engineers in New York have been working on similar technology to help teachers assess their impact on students (Alcorn, 2018).

Although powerful, facial recognition software still has the potential for error. A machine can misidentify a smile, for example, and attach the wrong motivation to the behavior—which, in turn, could prompt the user to make an incorrect assumption or misstep in addressing the behavior. Like any technology, facial recognition has its limits and drawbacks as well as benefits.

TEACHING FEATURE EXTRACTION

Students can learn how facial recognition works by physically acting out the algorithm in a game. Dr. Joshua Ho, a computer scientist working with CSIRO's ICT in Schools Program to integrate computer programming into math and science classes, suggests an activity for teaching the concept of feature extraction, or the conversion of data from an image into a series of quantitative or qualitative features that can be used to distinguish different objects within in the image (Ho, 2018).

Start with a class discussion on how we recognize faces by extracting key features from the images and matching them with what we know. Then give students a series of images—Ho uses Disney princesses—and have them practice breaking the pictures down into physical characteristics. Does she have long hair? What color is her dress? Is she holding anything? Students can use the answers to create a "database" of features, against which they can compare a new image to see which is the best match. For detailed instructions, read Ho's article on facial recognition in the classroom (**tinyurl.com/ycub4j9m**).

ACCESSIBILITY

Artificial intelligence can help visually impaired individuals see the world around them. Using computer vision, image and speech recognition, natural language processing, and machine learning, this technology reads text and answers questions, identifies emotions on people's faces, and describes surroundings to support the visually impaired user's ability to interact with their surroundings. Microsoft's Cognitive Services (**azure.microsoft.com/en-us/services/cognitive-services**) and Office Lens offer two features that employ this technology, Seeing AI and Immersive Reader (**tinyurl.com/y9zgcr3m**).

AUTONOMOUS VEHICLES

Autonomous vehicles have been making news headlines ever since Google purchased the company DeepMind in 2014, raising the possibility that they could translate the algorithm from a racing video game into a real, driverless vehicle. Although Google's **self-driving cars** have driven hundreds of thousands of miles since then, the technology is still far from viable.

Self-driving cars require a significant amount of preloaded data to function. The car needs to be able to compare pre-installed maps to information its sensors are detecting in real time, and details such as the height of traffic signals, the exact position of the curb, and building maps must be regularly updated within the car's computer. Because it takes an enormous amount of work to create and update these maps, the use of autonomous vehicles remains severely limited. This will most likely change as companies work to develop an intelligence high enough to guide the car without preprogrammed data (McFarland, 2015).

CREATIVE APPLICATIONS FOR AI

Creative pursuits are inspiring AI developers to cultivate more human ways of connecting. Drawing on expertise from comedians, novelists, poets, and animators, they are working to create personalities for AI tools. The Adobe Stock team provides extensive use of personal digital assistants that go beyond answering simple questions; Adobe engineers have referred to machine learning as coming to life.

The team has also conducted conversations with artists to see how they are using AI tools during the creative process. Visual search allows users to search for images similar to the original, while automated keywording generates keywords for images so artists don't need to tag photos they upload to the cloud (Adobe, 2017). Sensei, Adobe's AI tech, is integrated with the search feature in Photoshop, so artists can search their images in the cloud by typing in a keyword.

AI can help game developers create new video game content more quickly. Games such as the Doom franchise, which allows players to create their own levels to play, amass huge quantities of online data, which programmers can use to train algorithms to automatically generate new levels—saving video game creators the expense of manually creating content ("Emerging Technology from the arXiv," 2018). Computer scientists at Italy's Politecnico di Milano have designed an AI program that shoulders the majority of the difficult tasks of designing different levels of video game challenges, so designers and gamers are able to focus on the parts of the game they are most excited about (Robitzski, 2018).

AI and What It Means to Be Human

Now that AI is capable of emulating certain aspects of human thought, human learning, and human speech, machines are able to take on an increasing number of tasks that used to require human intelligence. What does this mean for our future?

Stephen Reid, Director of Immersive Minds, raises interesting questions about humanity's drive to harness technology to do our work for us. He says:

> The fact that the word "robot" comes directly and only from the Czech word for "slave" has always fascinated me. The idea that we as human beings cannot live and develop without using "slaves" to do whatever we can't or no longer want to. From horses to plough fields, people shipped from Africa and other countries, to

surveillance cameras, traffic lights (called robots in South Africa) and, now, AI. Even the process of thinking and learning is being turned into a "slave" process. Questions are: What happens when we have nothing left to do for ourselves? What is it we are seeking to achieve in the race to AI? Whatever makes us think we are so superior that enslavement or robotics and AI is ours to command?

When I land home tomorrow, a "robot" will check my passport. I will enter the country on the "yay" or "nay" of a machine. A coded machine, of course, but a machine nonetheless. If the machine has AI, and could make subjective as well as objective decisions, is my entry to my home country guaranteed?

Of course, this all sounds negative and plays to the AI naysayer narrative. I actually love the AI debate. But these points are well worth considering. (S. Reid, personal communication, May 1, 2018)

These are some of the questions artists have grappled with as they consider the impending arrival of AI. Their visions of AI in robotic form have given rise to a multitude of fears—of intelligent machines taking over, of human enslavement to technology, and even of people increasingly losing their humanity as machines get better at emulating it. The 2008 Pixar animated film *WALL-E* presents a cautionary tale demonstrating what might happen if we allow machines to start replacing too much of what makes us human, thereby impacting both human relationships and the environment. Throughout the film, robots WALL-E and EVA increasingly demonstrate human characteristics such as compassion, empathy, and sacrifice, while the humans in the film take on more robotic qualities. The robotic characters in *WALL-E* subvert our expectations of robots by exemplifying behaviors we associate with humans.

ANIMATED FILMS TO LAUNCH CLASSROOM DISCUSSIONS · · · · · · ·

The historic 1927 science fiction film *Metropolis* got people wondering about a future with machines that seemed human. How has humanity's image of human-like robots changed—or stayed the same—since then?

You can watch the following animated films with your students to help launch a classroom discussion on AI. Use the included activities and resources to adapt the learning for different classes and grade levels.

BIG HERO 6

Big Hero 6 explores design thinking, STEM learning, and the process of failure and iteration. It provides an excellent visual for collaboration, mentoring, and how mentoring and teaching can leave a legacy for students. Teachers can use this film to launch a discussion on ethics as students examine how the tools and innovations presented in the film could be used for positive impact—or in ways that destroy.

Activities and Resources

Did you know that the concept for an intelligent program to assess healthcare solutions, embodied in the *Big Hero 6* robot character Baymax, is actually a reality at Alder Hey Children's Hospital in Liverpool, England, and other hospitals throughout the country? This film may encourage us to consider: How can people and computers be connected so that, collectively, they are more intelligent than any single person, group, or computer?

Discuss the possibilities for AI in healthcare. Watch the video about enhancing patient care with cognitive computing at Alder Hey Children's Hospital (**youtu.be/mtYsbtTCVtY**). How is the analogy of the violin and violinist similar to humans and computers? Learn more about IBM Watson (**ibm.com/watson**).

Discuss trials and failure as they are featured in the movie. Explore the process of learning through failed attempts by watching and discussing the Crash Course Kids video "Succeed by Failing" (**youtu.be/TcUX6eNT2j4**).

Creative constraints such as requirements and limitations are a necessary part of the design process, and they can propel us to new heights of innovation. Help students understand the role of creative constraints in driving discovery and invention through this TED-Ed talk (**youtu.be/v5FL9VTBZzQ**). Find additional curriculum support in the Think, Dig Deeper, and Discuss sections of the TED-Ed website (**tiny.cc/gmiewy**).

WALL-E

WALL-E depicts the experiences of a trash compactor robot in a dystopian setting where humans have become passive and complacent, allowing machines to take over the aspects of life that require hard work. In this compelling and heartwarming film, humans have not maintained their personal health or the health of their planet. WALL-E meets EVA, a different type of robot, and both are dynamic characters who learn and grow through emotion. They use caring and loyalty to help snap the more robot-like human characters out of their apparent stupor.

Activities and Resources

Humans infer a huge amount of information through storytelling, which develops our ability to understand things in context. Use the silent film segments in *WALL-E* to practice developing inferential skills, and talk about how this is different from what machines can do. Have students point to the evidence in these silent film segments that led them to their conclusions. To assist in developing this process, use visual thinking strategies or access storytelling support (**storycenter.org/education**). Challenge students to convey story and human emotion by creating their own silent films. These could also be submitted to the International Youth Silent Film Festival (**makesilentfilm.com**). Explore the interplay between STEM and storytelling through Pixar in a Box (**khanacademy.org/partner-content/pixar**), a Khan Academy course that gives students a behind-the-scenes look at how Pixar artists draw upon math and science to tell stories.

WALL-E can serve as a launch pad for a debate in which students take a stance on the difference between robotics and AI, whether the robots in the film are AI, or nonverbal storytelling versus storytelling with words. *WALL-E* provides an opportunity to discuss what makes us uniquely human and different from machines. Note that at several points in the movie, it could be argued that the robots display more intelligence and human emotion than the humans around them. The film also features a dystopian caution about AI taking control through the antagonist robot called AUTO, inspired by the AI character in the classic film *2001: A Space Odyssey*. To help students understand debate skills and how to launch a debate based on a film, watch the Crash Course "How to Argue - Induction & Abduction" (**youtu.be/-wrCpLJl1XAw**).

Have students look for technology advancements seen in *WALL-E*, including AI features such as natural language processing. For examples of types of technology, find information on AI as it relates to *WALL-E* here: **tiny.cc/fqiewy**.

WALL-E can inspire an environmental study or a study on how AI could support a healthy lifestyle. Watch Crash Course Environment videos for older children (**youtu.be/5eTCZ9L834s**) and younger children (**youtu.be/SzcGTd8qWTg**).

Use *WALL-E* to inspire multidisciplinary projects that draw on science, technology, engineering, arts, and mathematics. Watch 13-year-old Renton Prep student Daniella's *WALL-E* project (**youtu.be/klmiGYhLwoQ**), inspired by recycled art and a study of simple machines and the engineering process.

· ·

History of AI

The investigation of intelligent machines dates further back than people new to AI may realize. To help the new generation understand what a long-term project AI is, Rodney Brooks, Panasonic Professor of Robotics (emeritus) at MIT, wrote a blog post updating his 1991 paper on the history of AI, since "to many it all seems so shiny and exciting and new." Of those, he adds, "it is exciting only" (Brooks, 2018).

Computer scientist Alan Turing began laying the groundwork for AI as early as 1948. Turing is best known for developing the Turing Test, which he introduced in "Computing Machinery and Intelligence" (Turing, 1950) to evaluate AI's ability to imitate human behavior. Using a 1950 version of instant messaging, a human would converse with a computer while a third party attempted to determine which conversant was the machine. Turing hoped that by the year 2000, a computer with 128MB of memory (he states it as binary digits) would have a 70% chance of fooling a person (Brooks, 2018).

ALAN TURING ·

Watch the Crash Course Video on Alan Turing: **tiny.cc/qyzywy**.

Consider introducing your older students to the 2014 film *The Imitation Game*. Discuss historical accuracies, ethics, social justice, and equality along with design thinking and solving real-world problems.

Connect this content with investigating the Global Goals (**globalgoals.org**) and which goals from Alan Turing's time still need work to make an impact by the year 2030.

· ·

A group of researchers are credited with first using the term "artificial intelligence" in 1955. In a proposal for Dartmouth University, (McCarthy et. al., 1955) they made a case for attempting to "find how to make machines use language, form abstractions and concepts, solve kinds of problems now reserved for humans, and improve themselves." By the middle of the 1960s, AI research was heavily funded by the Department of Defense, and the study of AI had begun to spread across the globe. As people continued searching for the correct problems to solve that would bring them closer to answering the questions needed to create artificial intelligence, sub-disciplines began to form, splintering AI research in so many directions that people couldn't keep on top of its sheer breadth. These subdisciplines included:

- planning
- problem-solving
- knowledge representation
- natural language processing
- search
- game playing
- expert systems
- neural networks
- machine inference
- statistical machine learning
- robotics
- mobile robotics
- simultaneous localization and mapping
- computer vision
- image understanding

But the AI boom didn't last. The complexity of the challenges involved in replicating human intelligence became increasingly evident in the early 1970s, and by 1974 the U.S. and British governments ended their exploratory AI research, ushering in what is referred to as an **AI winter**. AI researchers struggled to find funding for their projects until the early 1980s, when AI advancement surged again, its market reaching over a billion dollars by 1985. But 1987 brought another AI winter. As computational power increased in the late 1990s and early 2000s, however, artificial intelligence started to show promise in areas such as data mining and medical diagnosis, sparking interest in using AI to solve specific problems.

As researchers discovered new ways to leverage AI, the technology started making its way into businesses. By 2017, a survey suggested that one out of five companies used AI in some way, and nearly 85% believed AI would help them sustain or gain an advantage over competitors (Ransbotham, Kiron, Gerbert, & Reeves, 2017).

BEATING HUMANS AT THEIR OWN GAMES

IBM periodically pits "man against machine" in public challenges designed to attract workers to STEM fields (Best, 2013). The first computer to play chess and win over a reigning world chess champion was Deep Blue on May 11, 1997. The highly publicized event featured six chess matches between the IBM supercomputer, capable of analyzing 200 million chess moves a second, and world chess champion Garry Kasparov. Watch a short documentary about the match at **youtu.be/NJarxpYyoFI**.

The next challenge, in 2011, introduced the public to IBM Watson when the machine defeated two champions at the game show *Jeopardy*. Since then, Watson has expanded into healthcare and other industries.

In 2016, AlphaGo was the first computer program that used machine learning to beat a world champion Go player. The program was developed by Google's DeepMind, which has continued to improve since the match by playing millions of games against itself. According to the highest-ranked Go player from the Western world, "humans have accumulated knowledge that might tend to be more useful on the sides and corners of the board. AlphaGo 'has less of that bias, so it can make impressive moves in the center that are harder for us to grasp" (Chawn, 2017).

USING SWAY

Use this visual infographic from Live Science on the history of AI (**tiny.cc/o9iewy**) to start a discussion with your students about what they have heard regarding AI, and what is new to them. Have students work in teams to research the topics they haven't heard of before and create a project using multimedia or presentation tools. One recommended tool is Sway (**sway.com**).

Sway is a free tool built on machine learning algorithms to automatically create a visually appealing design so students can focus on creating content. Students can simultaneously coauthor content on sway on their mobile devices, laptops, or desktop computers. Machine learning features allow students to search for content that is Creative Commons licensed so there is no concern about copyright. Image searches are recommended based on text, and media can be embedded from other sources.

Take an introductory course for Sway here: **education.microsoft.com/gettrained/ introduction-to-sway**.

See an example of a collaborative class Sway based on experiential learning: **sway. com/bIb8UB34iPfAcJFV**.

The Current AI Season: How AI Is Being Used

People in the field talk about "AI seasons as periods of growth, excitement, and acceptance of advancing artificial intelligence. At times, however, the hype and overpromises of AI have exceeded the technology's ability to deliver, leading to AI winters. During these dry spells, funding decreases or becomes nonexistent as the general population loses interest in AI, and the hope of seeing this technology become a reality grows dim. As time passes and new advancements are made, the cycle of excitement and promise begins again, leading to a season of growth and advancement in the field. Those who have never experienced the period before an AI winter often perceive AI as something new and revolutionary, not realizing that AI seasons have been occurring since the 1950s. It may seem surprising that people have been tackling the challenge of AI for so long, and that each wave of excitement has resulted in similar predictions for the near future. But the more we discover about the complexity of human intelligence and learning, the more we recognize new lines of inquiry and research with AI.

In the current AI season, highly collaborative teams are working on solutions across multiple advancing fields. Developments in artificial intelligence are occurring within fields, including education, computer science, medical diagnosis, business and finance, aeronautics, defense, industry, media, telecommunications, and gaming.

AI WITH INTERDISCIPLINARY TEAMS IN THE MEDICAL FIELD

Nile Wilson wants to help people with neurologic damage regain their independence. A graduate student researcher completing her PhD in Bioengineering at the University of Washington as a part of the Center for Sensorimotor Neural Engineering, she aims to improve the quality and accessibility of technology that may grant people increased independence and more confidence to perform daily tasks by themselves, reducing reliance on caregivers (N. Wilson, personal communication, May 2, 2018).

Wilson works with a technology called a **brain-computer interface** (BCI). BCIs "acquire brain signals, analyze them, and translate them into commands that are relayed to output devices that carry out desired actions" (Shih, Krusienski, & Wolpawc, 2012). The technology is intended to help benefit people who have experienced neurologic damage due to conditions such as traumatic brain injuries (TBI), stroke, and spinal cord injuries. A lot goes into interfacing with the human body as researchers work toward that goal. One major hurdle is the reliable detection of particular brain wave patterns during BCI use. Although characteristic waveforms have been identified in the field, everyone's brain waves are different, and sometimes those signals defined in the literature are difficult to find. To combat this issue and allow for more a personalized BCI that works well for individual users, Wilson's team hopes to use AI to help identify particular brain wave patterns during BCI use (N. Wilson, personal communication, May 4, 2018).

Neuroscience-inspired AI, along with continued progress in the field of neuroscience, may greatly impact AI advancement. Improving BCIs demands intense collaboration from a broad interdisciplinary team that includes caregivers, clinicians, rehabilitation professionals, material science experts, philosophers for **neuroethics**, experts in social impact, computer scientists, and the individual using the end product. AI is one part of the solution, as is human intelligence that has the ability to transfer knowledge across domains (Bransford & Schwartz, 1999). Transferring learning from one setting or context to the next may happen with or without our awareness that it is happening. For humans, transfer of knowledge is a natural and intuitive part of learning. It is not as easy for machines to transfer learning across different contexts or apply that learning to a novel situation.

IBM WATSON

Since its famous *Jeopardy* victory, IBM Watson has been busy helping to diagnose medical conditions, providing feedback for medical professionals, and serving as an intelligent assistant for educators teaching mathematics. IBM Watson's Teacher Advisor (**teacheradvisor.org/landing**) is powered by AI to help direct educators to vetted content (Crozier, 2017).

IBM Watson has also partnered with Sesame Workshop (**sesameworkshop.org**) with the goal of using AI to support early literacy and vocabulary development for English Language Learners (ELL) and students just learning to read (Harris, 2017). The program allows children to move at their own pace and learn new words when they're ready, rather than being held to the same timing as everyone in the class. The results indicate student enthusiasm for learning new and larger words in a gamified setting. We know from research that early vocabulary development can provide a solid foundation for academic success.

TEACHER ADVISOR

For educators just beginning to use technology—or those who have been using it for a long time and are looking for high-quality math materials that are searchable by standards—Teacher Advisor (**teacheradvisor.org/landing**) is a great place to start. The free lesson-planning tool currently supports K-8 math instruction.

Hear educators talk about using Teacher Advisor with a range of skill and ability levels: **youtu.be/Kzp3YuC_Dr8**.

MIA LEARNING

Mia Learning's (**mialearning.com**) voice chatbot supports elementary and middle school students in their independent reading. Secret Agent Mia enlists students in her mission to end boredom. She helps them decide what they want to get out of reading, guides them toward choosing books that match their interests and abilities, and coaches them on how to decide where, when, and with whom to read. During her conversations with students, she offers personalized book recommendations and coaching while gleaning insights to help educators and parents find new ways of engaging children in reading. She strives to increase both students' and educators' agency and autonomy.

Mia's approach is supported by a strong body of experimental research that demonstrates how increasing students' motivation to read, and the amount they read, has strong causal effects on their growth in reading ability. What Mia knows about readers and reading is informed by a taskforce of top literacy researchers, classroom teachers, librarians, community literacy leaders, and children's playwrights who bring the character and story to life (D. Cambridge, Personal Communication, 2018).

As STEM professionals continue to search for the "loose screw" that will unlock true artificial intelligence—and as industries across the board continue to employ AI to augment human performance—we can expect to see further advancements in field. In the meantime, existing AI technologies are constantly collecting new data, learning from it, and improving themselves. While a future in which intelligent robots interact the way children like Cub and Leila expect them to remains a distant dream, the hope of that reality is continually being renewed.

REFLECTING ON AI ·

- If AI increasingly becomes a part of our everyday lives (Lin, 2015), how will that influence careers and higher education for the children who will graduate in the year 2030 (Holzapfel, 2018)? Read more about how technology can empower the class of 2030 (**tinyurl.com/y7ghgsql**) and what skills students will need to be life-ready (**tinyurl.com/y9db53mc**).

- How might AI be unintentionally amplifying bias in education and other industries, and how might that affect your students in the future?

- Without context regarding the challenges educators face on a daily basis, and without knowledge of AI as it currently exists in society, bias can slip in and lead to unintended results. What do you need to be vigilant about to help minimize bias?

- Can a computer currently think and behave like a human? If it cannot, how can machines augment human capability and still maintain a balance between cultural traditions and modern innovations?

The next chapter begins to discuss these questions and will give you a chance to see how other educators around the world are thinking about AI. As you go through this book, use your own prior knowledge and context to consider how humans think, make decisions, work, and learn when trying to solve problems or accomplish a task.

· ·

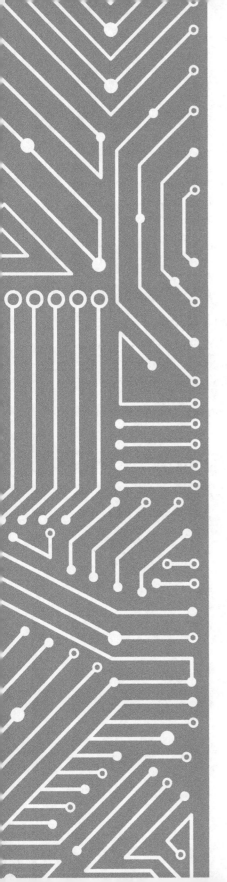

CHAPTER 2
Preparing Students for the Future

Conversations with Experts

DRAMATIS PERSONAE

JARED ZIMMERMAN: Design lead at Google

MICHELLE ZIMMERMAN: Author and educator

SCENE

Jared is having a conversation with the author about AI and how he would describe it to educators.

TIME: May 2018

ACT I

Scene 2

SETTING: The internet, connecting Hawaii and Washington though conversation

AT RISE: Jared is chatting on Facebook Messenger from a mobile phone in Hawaii with the author in Washington, who is also communicating via iPhone. Both converse using predictive models, a form of machine learning; autocomplete for the keyboard; and deep learning. Machine learning assists with keystrokes on a smartphone, facilitating communication that isn't face to face.

MICHELLE: What do you think educators should know about AI?

JARED: AI is a tool like any other. It isn't magic dust you sprinkle on things. For the moment, it can only do tasks a child would do, but quicker and in parallel. Basically, it gives you tens of thousands of six-year-olds doing something over and over again. Very specialized six-year-olds. It's as if you can only train each six-year-old to do one thing.

The computer program AlphaGo (Chan 2017) can beat any human in the world at Go, but it can't play Tic-Tac-Toe.

Artificial general intelligence (AGI) or "general AI" isn't really a thing yet. It just means an AI that can handle a new situation without training.

At this point we have algorithms and machine learning.

AI is a catch-all umbrella term.

End Scene 2

Today's students will live and work with AI. To succeed in their future jobs—regardless of the field they choose—they need to learn how to both maximize AI's capabilities and transcend its limits. As children progress from their conception of AI as intelligent robots to an understanding of how machines can replicate aspects of human intelligence, they expand their ability to effectively employ these tools in their own lives.

Because AI is advancing so rapidly, it is difficult to predict its impact on students' future work. Some fear that AI will take all of our jobs. Others argue that AI will create more jobs than it displaces, opening new opportunities today's students can't begin to imagine. In either case, as AI continues to take on more tasks that used to require a human, students will need to navigate a constantly changing job market in which a valuable talent today could become automated tomorrow. In an article for Getting Smart entitled "Staying Ahead of the Robots: What Grads Should Know and Be Able to Do" (**tiny.cc/37j4wy**), Tom Vander Ark shared the findings of a recent Pew Report on the future of jobs:

> *Machines are eating humans' job talents. And it's not just about jobs that are repetitive and low-skill. Automation, robotics, algorithms and artificial intelligence (AI) in recent times have shown they can do equal or sometimes even better work than humans who are dermatologists, insurance claims adjusters, lawyers, seismic testers in oil fields, sports journalists and financial reporters, crew members on guided-missile destroyers, hiring managers, psychological testers, retail salespeople, and border patrol agents. Moreover, there is growing anxiety that technology developments on the near horizon will crush the jobs of the millions who drive cars and trucks, analyze medical tests and data, perform middle management chores, dispense medicine, trade stocks and evaluate markets, fight on battlefields, perform government functions, and even replace those who program software—that is, the creators of algorithms. (Vander Ark, 2017)*

The pending changes to the future job landscape require educators to revisit learning outcomes. Vander Ark went on to share a review of outcome frameworks—shown in Table 2.1—including the 20 MyWays competencies from Next Generation Learning Challenges (**myways.nextgenlearning.org**), Tony Wagner's seven survival skills (**tonywagner.com/7-survival-skills**), the Hewlett Foundation's goals for deeper learning (**hewlett.org/strategy/deeper-learning**), the Collaborative for Academic Social and Emotional Learning (**casel.org**), and the World Economic Forum's top ten skills for 2020 (**tiny.cc/o6j4wy**).

Table 2.1 Learning outcomes needed to support students in future careers

NGLC MyWays	Tony Wagner	Deeper Learning	CASEL	E&Y 2020
Critical thinking & problem-solving	Critical thinking & problem-solving	Learning how to think critically and solve problems		Complex problem-solving, critical thinking
Creativity & entrepreneurship	Curiosity & imagination	Creativity		Creativity
Developing personal relationships	Collaboration across networks, leading by influence	Working collaboratively	Social awareness	People management, coordination
Social skills & responsibility			Relationship skills	Emotional intelligence
Navigating each step of the journey	Assessing & analyzing info		Decision making	Judgement, decision making
Positive mindsets	Initiative & entrepreneurship	Developing an academic mindset	Self-awareness	Service orientation
Academic behaviors	Agility & adaptability			Negotiation, cognitive flexibility
Communication & collaboration	Oral & written communication	Communicating effectively		
Self-direction & perseverance, learning strategies		Directing one's own learning	Self-management	
Content & global knowledge		Mastering rigorous academic content		
Info, media & tech; career tech & practical skills				

Source: Vander Ark, 2017 (**tiny.cc/37j4wy**).

Note the overlap and emphasis on "human" skills such as creativity, interpersonal skills, and self-awareness. According to Vander Ark, "the rise of artificial intelligence (AI) — code that can learn and act based on observed patterns in data sets—is driving a new shift in value with a focus on sentiments more intrinsic to the human experience: thinking, creativity, and problem-solving" (Vander Ark, 2017).

UNDERSTANDING AI ·

Read the Pew Research Center report "The Future of Jobs and Job Training" at **tinyurl.com/y94ygdxg**.

Read predictions from experts, compiled by Pew Research Center and Elon's Imagining the Internet Center, about jobs and job training in 2026 at **tiny. cc/3nk4wy**.

· ·

AI can perform many of the tasks that used to lie firmly within the human domain—but it can't do everything. As educators prepare students to work side by side with this powerful tool, it is important to recognize that the in-demand job skills of the future will be those that begin wherever AI's capabilities end. Now that machines are capable of learning, so too will students need to develop the habit of constantly learning, growing, and making connections across multiple domains if they are to work effectively in collaboration with AI.

Comparing Human Learning and AI

Machines, like children, learn though repetition. If you have taught a class of six-year-olds, Jared's analogy from the chapter's opening scene may have made you laugh or reminded you of young children incessantly repeating the same task or behavior. If you have had a six-year-old child of your own, you may remember listening to the same song repeatedly, reading the same book for the hundredth time, or watching the same movie until you've both memorized the entire dialog.

Within that repetition, learning happens. A 2011 study on storybook repetition, published in the journal *Frontiers in Psychology,* demonstrates that "children who heard the same stories repeatedly retained words at significantly greater than chance levels." The study concludes that its findings are consistent with recent research that shows rereading the same picture books and rewatching the same television programs facilitates learning (Horst, Parsons & Bryan, 2011). It may be in that repetition specifically that learning continues to occur by identifying patterns, finding connections, developing inference, and connecting with human emotion through storytelling (Tokuhama-Espinosa, 2011; Medina, 2008).

Although Google design lead Jared Zimmerman isn't an educator, his analogy in Scene 2 demonstrates that machine learning is doing just that—it is learning much as a young child would. But repetition is where the similarity between human and machine learning ends. While human memory acquires information through the senses, then stores and later retrieves that information, machine learning acquires data from various inputs that can include text, images, sound, and touch. For humans, the way the information is received—and which senses are involved—has an influence on how information is processed and remembered (Baddeley, 1990, p. 9; Medina, 2008; Kopell & Greenberg, 2008; Tsukiura & Cabeza, 2008; Groenwegen, 2007). As a result, there are aspects of learning that are still considered uniquely human, and that machines are not yet capable of doing, such as transferring learning from one setting to another—or storytelling.

COMMUNICATION THROUGH STORYTELLING

Owen Suskind was diagnosed with regressive autism and was unable to speak as a child until he and his family discovered a unique way to communicate by immersing themselves in the world of Disney animated films.

Share the story about how storytelling helped Owen communicate through finding and repeating a scene in a Disney movie (**tiny.cc/8yk4wy**). Your students may also enjoy the documentary film, *Life Animated*, based on Owen's story. The film and curriculum guide are available here: **lifeanimateddoc.com**.

Discuss with students how Owen and his family learned to communicate through storytelling and repetition. Compare this with the way AlphaGo learned, as described in the *Atlantic* article "The AI that has Nothing to Learn from Humans," and the quote: "Generally the way humans learn Go is that we have a story" (Chan, 2017). Read the article at **tinyurl.com/y9puanus**.

Emotion plays a role in human learning. For example, take the story of Cub and Leila from the opening scene to Chapter 1: based on their prior experiences and knowledge, the children applied their learning to a novel situation as they attempted to find a solution to their unmet goal of interacting with the robot. For young children, exploration is a necessity and can even evoke feelings of joy. Positive or negative emotions, if innate psychological needs are met, can facilitate or forestall authentic motivation to persist when the task becomes difficult (Ryan & Deci, 2000). A machine can continue to collect data without emotion influencing the process, but it also lacks the element of curiosity that propels children to explore and learn.

John Medina is a developmental molecular biologist and research consultant. An affiliate professor of bioengineering at the University of Washington School of Medicine, and *New York Times* bestselling author of the book, *Brain Rules* (**brainrules.net**), he explains how curiosity drives learning:

> *Most developmental psychologists believe that a child's need to know is a drive as pure as diamonds and as distracting as chocolate. Even though there is no agreed-upon definition of curiosity in cognitive neuroscience, I couldn't agree more. I firmly believe that if children are allowed to remain curious, they will continue to deploy their natural tendencies to discover and explore until they are 101. This is something my mother seemed to know instinctively.*

> *For little ones, discovery brings joy. Like an addictive drug, exploration creates the need for more discovery so that more joy can be experienced. It is a straight-up reward system that, if allowed to flourish, will continue into the school years. As children get older, they find that learning not only brings them joy, but it also brings them mastery. Expertise in specific subjects breeds the confidence to take intellectual risks. If these kids don't end up in the emergency room, they may end up with a Nobel Prize (Medina, 2008).*

Watch Dr. Medina talk about "Theory of Mind" at **youtu.be/cdjWAkIxNMo**.

Beyond drawing upon prior knowledge and experiencing joy while discovering more about the robot, Leila and Cub conversed with each other, using their hands and speech (Vygotsky, 1987) to build further understanding as they took in sensory information (Baddeley, 1990). Vygotsky's (1987) fundamental idea was that human learning is a complex process in which both social situations and sensory modalities engage and interact. He spoke of "the unity of perception, speech, and action, which ultimately produces internalization of the visual field" (p. 26). Hooker, Verosky, Gemine, Knight, and D'Esposito (2010) also identified the implication of the front part of the brain, called frontal cortex, as it relates to stimuli from social interaction. In socially mediated learning, it is important to learn to examine a situation from another person's point of view while "taking into account that the other person acts and reacts to a situation based on beliefs, goals, and intentions that may be different from one's own." This process is referred to as mentalizing, or "**Theory of Mind**" (p. 101). Cognitive empathy is a human emotion that "includes mentalizing skills such as perspective-taking" (p. 100). Storytelling—watching and listening to stories—helps build perspective-taking and empathy in humans. Machines don't yet have that capability.

Children take in a massive amount of sensory information as they learn, and their brains build and strengthen pathways in the process (Kopell & Greenberg, 2008; Turgeon, 2012). Social contexts provide important input to the brain as the sensory information they receive from external sources in the environment is processed in association areas in the brain and reaches an area called the basal ganglia, which generates a motor response to sensory information (Kopell & Greenberg, 2008). As Leila and Cub explored possible interactions with the robot, they were engaging in what Vygotsky refers to as sociocultural learning. The two young people interacted with each other by speaking, using their hands (motor response) to test their ideas. The information they received from a variety of sources helped them create a series of questions and to relate their previous experience with and information received from stories and movies (mostly science fiction).

Paul Allen (2011) points out that humans learn differently than machines as they grow from infants to adults. They acquire a general knowledge about the world, then they refine and add to that knowledge as they experience different contexts—as we saw Cub and Leila doing. Machines, on the other hand, have a long way to go before they can show the same type of intelligence as a human across a wide range of contexts and novel situations, rather than a depth of expertise in one particular domain or field.

CASE STUDY ·

The AI revolution is co-occurring alongside another major scientific development: the emergence of citizen science. As scientists continue to bump up against AI's limits, they're increasingly enlisting everyday citizens to help observe, record, and process massive amounts of information. Through a combination of advanced technology and human ingenuity, they are making new discoveries that weren't possible until now.

The program PICK Education (**pickedu.com**), using an educational philosophy that challenges traditional modes of teaching, harnesses the social side of human learning through citizen science. The program's main tenet is to develop methodology to implement data analysis in a learning environment that impacts current challenges found around the world. Within the program, teachers and students alike take on the role of research scientists by contributing to real-world scientific inquiry and investigation. Everyone involved in these collaborations—students and professionals alike—has benefited from this approach. Robert Thornell, EdD, deputy superintendent of curriculum and instruction for Ector County ISD, wrote in a personal communication (May 12, 2018) about two students who received full four-year scholarships at Southern Methodist University (SMU) to continue in biomedical studies. Both the students and the university noted that the teenagers' experiences in PICK Education offered them learning opportunities that placed them far ahead of their peers.

Jason Osborne, chief innovation officer for Ector County ISD in Texas, is working with K-12 science coordinator Ashley Bryant to develop and implement PICK Education. A White House Champion of Change whose work has been recognized in

Figure 2.1
PICK Education programs, like this one developed by Jason Osborne in Ector County, Texas, introduce students to citizen science. Photo credit: Gabriela Granado.

major publications from *Scientific American* to *National Geographic*, Osborne poses an interesting question: what if we expanded students' learning communities beyond their teachers, principals, and counselors to include peers, college students, university faculty, and researchers? He sees citizen science as a way to do that. Below are some examples of citizen science programs educators can leverage in the classroom.

Paleo Quest: Osborne co-founded Paleo Quest, a nonprofit citizen science organization whose mission is to advance the sciences of paleontology and geology through research, exploration, and science education. Paleo Quest is an original, collaborative platform that brings together professional-amateurs, professionals, and citizen scientists in a variety of disciplines, providing a greenhouse for scientific innovation. The organization's novel approach to science has helped participants identify and answer unique scientific and methodological questions in paleontology and stratigraphy.

Project Brain STEM: Through Project Brain STEM (**youtu.be/cOiZf8ViqaA**), teachers and students can assist researchers in identifying neural structures within a drosophila fly brain data set. By employing students as an extension of the lab, researchers can utilize students' work to map the brain at a much faster rate than before. This, in turn, allows the science to progress at a faster rate. Students benefit by learning about the structures of the brain as well as scientific processes, all of which are required by state standards.

SharkFinder: School partnerships with industry, universities, and research institutes aren't limited to secondary students. K-5 learners have also contributed to science thanks to a program called SharkFinder, in which students help discover micro-fossils that may be scientifically significant. Much like Project Brain STEM, SharkFinder allows for a greater mass of data to be analyzed, which has led to an exponential growth in discoveries of first occurrences of species. Perhaps its most notable effect on students and teachers is allowing the seamless weaving of cross-curricular content. Students learn about science, social studies, and mathematics while also employing reading and writing skills, making SharkFinder a true example of STEM learning.

Learn more about PICK Education at **exploring pickedu.com**. Watch a report on what the PICK Education program does and its potential for all schools at **youtu.be/gLhTOWKICmY**.

(Adapted from Obama White House Archives (Osborne, 2015) (**tinyurl.com/ybdvfj4u**) and J. Osborne personal communication, May 9–13, 2018).

REFLECTING ON AI ·

- From what we have learned so far, what indicates learning that currently is uniquely human, and what can machines do well under the right circumstances?

- In the *Atlantic* article, Redmond—the highest-ranked Go player in the Western world—notes that games with AlphaGo somehow feel "alien." "There's some inhuman element in the way AlphaGo plays," he says, "which makes it very difficult for us to just even sort of get into the game." What elements do humans use to help them play that a machine does not?

- If AlphaGo can beat another human at a complex game but cannot play Tic-Tac-Toe, what can it not do that Owen Suskind—and six-year-olds—can do?

- How does the lack of emotion in machine learning limit AI's capabilities, especially with regard to communication?

· ·

How AI Machine Learning Works

While children's natural curiosity often propels learning, machines must be trained. In an episode of Google Cloud Platform's *AI Adventures* video series, developer Yufeng Guo breaks this training process down into seven steps.

1. Gathering data

2. Data preparation

3. Choosing a model

4. Training

5. Evaluation

6. Parameter tuning

7. Prediction

The first step is *gathering data* to be input and used to develop an AI carrier (model). This is referred to as "training data." The quantity and quality of the data gathered will directly determine the capability of your predictive model.

According to Nathan Laurie, a graduate student studying materials science and engineering with a data science option at the University of Washington, *data preparation* can be, by far, the most time-consuming step in developing machine learning, since data needs to be formatted in a way the algorithm can read it. With large amounts of data to input, there may be multiple sources that need reformatting. Laurie describes this as the "unglamorous part" of machine learning. He emphasizes that, as much as possible, it is important to communicate details on how to best format the data from the beginning (N. Laurie, personal communication, 2018).

Next, the data is loaded to a suitable place such as cloud storage. Preparing the data also includes randomizing the data, then splitting it into two groups. One of the groups is for training, and the other is for evaluation once the model is trained. Sometimes data preparation also includes purging duplicate data or background noise.

The third step involves *choosing a model*. There are many different types of machine learning models, depending on the type of question you want the machine to be able to answer. A binary classification model, for example, teaches a machine to predict binary outcomes such as whether or not an email is spam. A regression model predicts numerical values, such as what the temperature will be tomorrow. Certain models are best suited for certain types of data. For example, facial recognition software uses a model geared toward image data, whereas a chatbot might require a text-based model.

The bulk of developing machine learning occurs during the *training* step. During this phase, data is used to incrementally improve how accurately the model predicts real-world data outcomes. Weights and biases should be considered and, where appropriate, updated as part of this step.

The fifth step is *evaluation*. The original data has been split into two groups, and the unused data will be employed to determine if the model is effective at predicting—in other words, how the model will perform in the real world.

During the sixth step, known as *parameter tuning* or *hyperparameter tuning*, the programmer fine-tunes the training process by examining parameters such as how many times they ran through the training set or how much they were able to improve the machine's capabilities at each training step.

The seventh and final step is *prediction*, a determination of how well the model predicts or infers what you want to know without the assistance of human judgment.

TEACHING A COMPUTER TO GENERATE NATURAL LANGUAGE · · ·

To make a conversation feel human (natural), AI's responses should make sense within the context of the dialogue. In other words, the language needs to be used correctly. Researchers and developers first consider how a human would respond. Another consideration is: what information needs to be summarized so it doesn't become repetitive and robotic?

Figuring out what to say and how to say it is done with stable and predictable rules that require a lot of information—an approach that is not scalable to different contexts, languages, or outputs. For example, if rules were written for a machine to respond by giving a weather report, it requires new set of rules to deliver the report in a different language. This becomes a daunting task that isn't scalable.

By giving a model examples of data and language it needs to generate, the hope is that machine learning will form its own rules, with the freedom to be creative. Laurie refers to this as "unsupervised learning"—the learning algorithm is allowed to develop connections between unlabeled data. These connections are usually hidden to a human observer or with traditional data analysis techniques (N. Laurie, personal communication, 2018). For this to work, the model needs to be shown many examples to draw upon when answering questions. If successful, it isn't necessary to write as many rules; machine learning does the rest. This is one of the goals of machine learning.

· ·

GETTING STARTED WITH AI IN THE CLASSROOM · · · · · · · · · · · · · · ·

Tensor Flow Playground: Play with machine learning training and parameters in a browser-based sandbox simulation. You can't break it: **playground.tensorflow.org**.

Watch the Cloud AI Adventures video on the 7 Steps of Machine Learning: **youtu.be/nKW8Ndu7Mjw**.

· ·

Making Machine Learning More Complex

Paul Allen (2011) wrote an article that describes why we have a long way to go before machines can show the same type of intelligence as humans across a wide range of contexts and novel situations. Rather, machine learning currently offers a depth of expertise in one particular domain or field. Allen described the human brain compared with AI:

The complexity of the brain is simply awesome. Every structure has been precisely shaped by millions of years of evolution to do a particular thing, whatever it might be. It is not like a computer, with billions of identical transistors in regular memory arrays that are controlled by a CPU with a few different elements. In the brain every individual structure and neural circuit has been individually refined by evolution and environmental factors. The closer we look at the brain, the greater the degree of neural variation we find. Understanding the neural structure of the human brain is getting harder as we learn more. Put another way, the more we learn, the more we realize there is to know, and the more we have to go back and revise our earlier understandings. We believe that one day this steady increase in complexity will end—the brain is, after all, a finite set of neurons and operates according to physical principles. (Allen, 2011)

Researchers attempting to build human-like intelligence typically have tried to build systems with deep knowledge of narrow areas, with the goal of combining them to simulate the way humans learn. More recently, AI researchers have theorized about ways to model the complex phenomena that allow humans to remain flexible in uncertainty, to have contextual sensitivity, to understand variance in rules of thumb, to self-reflect, and to receive flashes of inspiration (2011).

UNDERSTANDING AI

A spam filter is an example of a linear model. But what happens when it's not that simple? **Deep neural networks (DNN)** help data scientists adapt more complex data sets and better generalize to new data. Their multiple layers allow for more complex data sets, but the drawback is that neural networks take longer to train and are larger in size, with less interpretability. Getting all the parameters just right can be daunting.

To learn more about deep neural networks, watch the Cloud AI Adventures video here: **youtu.be/s0JvhHr3r8k**.

Watch a six-minute video, "What is Artificial Intelligence (or Machine Learning)?": **youtu.be/mJeNghZXtMo**.

As we can see, AI researchers cannot fully succeed at imitating human intelligence without a deep understanding of how the brain works, from cognitive and developmental psychology to biochemistry and neuroscience—an endeavor that will require scientists from many different fields to work together. To that end, the Allen Institute for Brain Science, founded in 2003, has expanded from its "initial pursuit of understanding the brain to encompass an investigation of the inner workings of cells and the funding of transformative scientific ideas around the world" (Allen Institute for Brain Science, 2018). Its hope is that by better understanding how the brain works, we might learn something about how to advance artificial intelligence.

Implications for Future Careers in Which AI Is Used

In this section, you will find examples of businesses and career fields that will influence and propel the direction of AI. We'll look at what influencers such as business and education leaders are doing now in the AI field. To help students to understand this emerging field, it's important for teachers and administrators to stay up to date on the subject.

The following five companies and potential career paths have been selected from this author's conversations with graduate students and professionals currently working in the field. Each represents an example of an occupation that utilizes machine learning. In these examples, machine learning is leveraged for animation, finding chemical and molecular patterns, quick object identification that is faster than human perception (for security purposes), and identifying brain waves.

PIXAR ANIMATION STUDIOS

Although 2018 is supposed to be a year of major progress for AI, a recent article, "What Pixar Can Teach Us about AI & Machine Learning" (Angelani, 2018) reflects back on 2004 and asserts that Pixar set a standard with its film, *The Incredibles*. During the main characters' fight with a robot known as the Omnidroid, the machine learns while continuing to fight in real time, demonstrating the use of both supervised and unsupervised data. Supervised algorithms support learning from the past in order to analyze new data. Unsupervised data is capable of making inferences from new datasets. Angelani explains that because the Omnidroid used both, it was ahead of its time.

UNDERSTANDING AI ·

Read the full article on what Angelani says Pixar can teach us about AI and Machine Learning through *The Incredibles*: **tinyurl.com/y7q8llhn**.

· ·

Moving beyond what was imagined and animated in 2004, today Pixar Animation Studios is using AI extensively and publishing papers on the outcomes. Pixar in a Box, a Khan Academy course that demonstrates how Pixar filmmakers draw upon traditional school subjects such as math, science, and the arts in their everyday work, is one of the most beautifully designed Science, Technology, Engineering, Arts, and Mathematics (STEAM) programs available. It provides a clear connection to careers and applications for animated films.

To help prepare young people for careers at companies such as Pixar, Pixar in a Box allows learners to explore and create "models" of different phenomena. (This is demonstrated in the character modeling activity in Figure 2.2.) For example, users can model water and hair via particle systems and explore the physics behind those models. Similarly, they can build a model and explore its mathematics. Each segment of Pixar in a Box includes real stories from animators, researchers, and scientists that inspire young people and help them learn about careers they (and their teacher) may not know exist. A module on storytelling is included.

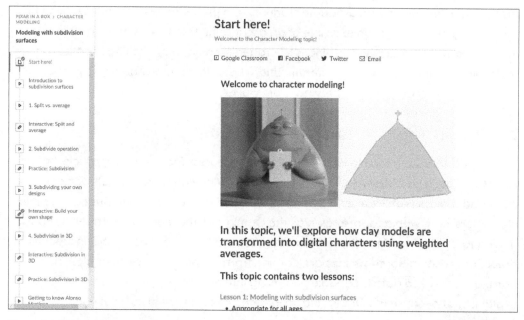

Figure 2.2 Learners can explore character modeling with Pixar in a Box.

TEACHING STEAM THROUGH ANIMATION · · · · · · · · · · · · · · · ·

Pixar in a Box is a free resource and curriculum for educators to use in the classroom now. Pixar in a Box is produced in collaboration with Khan Academy: **khanacademy.org/partner-content/pixar**.

· ·

In May 2018, Pixar in a Box cocreator Tony DeRose explained how Pixar is beginning to investigate ways that AI can support animation. He shared with me their first published paper on the topic, presented last summer at the Special Interest Group on Computer Graphics and Interactive Techniques (SIGGRAPH) conference. The paper describes a specific application of machine learning for rendering, or the process of using a computer program generate an image from a 3D or 2D model (**graphics.pixar.com/library/MLDenoisingB/index.html**).

MATERIAL SCIENCES AND ENGINEERING

According to Laurie, machine learning is "used everywhere." He explained that you can give descriptors to a machine learning algorithm, and it will find correlations between them that otherwise would be impossible to detect. He described a scenario application for 3D printing a mesh support for the human ankle that provides stiffness in certain places to prevent specific movements while still allowing general mobility. A 3D printer creates objects using a nozzle that moves around in a preprogrammed pattern, building up layers of plastic. The route it takes—and where it leaves gaps—determine the shape of the resulting object. The problem is trying to design a route the printer can take to achieve the exact thickness needed at each point. With machine learning, you can teach the model the outcomes of some nozzle routes and then tell it to build the desired ankle support. Students who go on to work in fields involving computer-assisted design and 3D printing may one day rely on such AI solutions to help them overcome challenges they face on the job.

Another example of machine learning in material sciences is the ability to predict the properties of materials and molecules. As we learned from the seven basic steps for machine learning, one of the goals is to be able to accurately predict outcomes or solutions. Nathan pointed out that it is not a good use of resources to go through one by one and experimentally determine, for example, which molecules are suitable candidates for a biofuel. He asserted that machine learning is an effective tool for narrowing down which molecules scientists should look at.

Finally, Nathan said, "The thing I find interesting is that even though you can get crazy accurate nonlinear regression, the 'solution' is not a solution. It doesn't give any insight into the physics of the problem. You can make it learn physics, but it's not learning physics. It just learns outcomes" (N. Laurie, personal communication, May 8, 2018).

We can think of this "lack of insight" as similar to children who learn math algorithms well enough to repeat the process, even scoring high on a test, without understanding the concepts behind them. When presented with a novel situation that prevents them from simply repeating the pattern, they are unable to arrive at an accurate solution. Similarly, a student who has memorized words but doesn't know what they mean may sound like they are reading fluently even though they cannot comprehend the passage or transfer the knowledge.

When I asked Nathan what he wishes educators knew, he said,

> Machine learning or AI in general isn't a free lunch. Lots of machine learning is from experimental data, so the data has to be. . .'good.' Just because some data is published doesn't mean it's good, unfortunately, even with proper procedure and proper science. With adding more descriptors to your data to predict something, you're adding experimental noise. Noise always exists with any measurement. You're also obfuscating the physical insight. Now there's one more descriptor that could be meaningless. Since you gain no physical insight with machine learning, it's hard to see if you're wrong or not. (N. Laurie, personal communication, May 8, 2018).

UNDERSTANDING AI

Read the article "Data Science: Accelerating Innovation and Discovery in Chemical Engineering" to find out more about the statistical, machine learning, and visualization tools available to chemical engineers: **tinyurl.com/y8p89m3g**.

DEFENSE FIELD

Major Ryan Shelhorse is an F-22 pilot in the U.S. Air Force. On May 8, 2018, I asked him if he uses AI in his work. He told me the military is in the early stages of human-machine teaming, but there is still a long way to go. He pointed out that the vision is there, but the science for artificial intelligence is too far off. In his opinion, giving machines the ability to think autonomously could have serious implications. "Once you train a machine to think for itself, where and how deep does it go?" His stance was direct: "Humans need to be in the loop. Always."

He is involved with a team charged with creating a human-machine teaming process. Using machine learning will allow them to fuse multiple nodes of information into a single output for the end-user to determine whether an aircraft is friend or foe. He said,

> In the fighter community, we focus a major effort on identifying all aircraft flying that could affect our mission. The idea is that there are multiple systems across multiple domains fusing into one data center that is working to identify an aircraft. When we can identify an aircraft earlier and more accurately, we are able to take advantage of an important concept in maneuver warfare. Battlefield commanders (e.g., fighter pilots) are able to decide and act quicker than the enemy because they've already observed and oriented their forces against the enemy. When battlefield commanders maintain this initiative and are able to communicate their intent to fielded forces, overall risk to the mission will be mitigated and reduced because the enemy is reacting versus acting.

He said that the possibilities of AI could be endless, but emphasized again that "there needs to be a way to shut it down," or to ensure a human is driving the whole process so that the international Law of Armed Conflict (LOAC) principles of necessity, distinction, and proportionality are maintained (**loacblog.com/loac-basics/4-basic-principles**).

When I asked what Major Shelhorse would say to educators about how best to prepare their learners for the future, he said, "Take a more proactive approach in figuring out the best way each of your students learn." This is a nuance that is still unique to humans— and that nuance can inspire passion and motivation to persist when things get difficult.

UNDERSTANDING AI ·

Explore the implications of using AI in autonomous weapon systems (AWS): **tinyurl.com/y7vnnwfo**.

Read about how the U.S. Air Force is using machine learning to identify the difference between friend and foe aircrafts more quickly and accurately: **tinyurl.com/ycdqu523**

Find out how the Air Force is prepping its F-22 for 2060, with new sensors, radar, avionics, and AI: **tinyurl.com/y8v9fyp2**.

Learn how aviator training is changing to make pilots more accustomed to using a wide range of technology: **tinyurl.com/y8yebtfd**.

· ·

A DARPA FOR EDUCATION

Global conflict and war have impacted humanity in a multitude of ways. Organizations such as the Defense Advanced Research Projects Agency (DARPA, **darpa.mil**) have been influential in developing technologies that are used in mainstream society today, such as automated voice recognition and GPS receivers small enough to be embedded in a mobile device.

Russell Shilling, a retired U.S. Navy captain and aerospace experimental psychologist, wrote an article for *Scientific American* proposing the creation a DARPA for Education (**tinyurl.com/ydd9fm9q**). "Unlike traditional basic or applied research, the DARPA method resides in a category that the late science policy researcher Donald E. Stokes introduced in his 1997 book, *Pasteur's Quadrant*," he said (Shilling, 2015). *Pasteur's Quadrant* is named after Louis Pasteur, who applied basic research to solve specific and immediate problems. During an event called EdFoo, which brought together 500 researchers, educators, and innovators at Google Headquarters in February, 2016, Shilling talked in personal conversations about the gap between lab research and practice, as well as the process for tackling larger challenges the way DARPA does. For DARPA, every project is a moon shot. Although the final goal is clear, there is flexibility in the approach, and the possibilities for research abound. For example, could a digital tutor powered by artificial intelligence adapt to a learner over the course of his or her education from preschool through college? Can similar technologies be developed to support or enhance ongoing learning throughout a person's life, outside the bounds of formal education? How can these technologies support a fluid understanding of learner progress and mastery, rather than waiting for a final assessment at the end of a course of study?

In his article, Russell talked about the need to bring together "the most innovative teams of researchers, professional developers, and educators to tackle problems as a whole" (2015). He concluded that when people maintain a goal and vision for improving educational outcomes, the vision can be adjusted. Back in 1968, DARPA researchers wouldn't have been able to predict what the internet would become. The people working to solve challenges in education won't know what's possible until they join together to make things happen.

UNDERSTANDING AI ·

Did you know that without DARPA, we might not have the internet—or even this book? Many of DARPA's advancements in technology are now used by the general public. Read about it here: **tinyurl.com/3pugj9f**.

ACCESSIBILITY THROUGH BIOMEDICAL ADVANCES

In the biomedical field, machine learning offers new ways of improving accessibility for people with a wide range of disabilities. Even though the dream of high-functioning, accessible brain-computer interaction has not yet been realized yet, new technologies are emerging to assist people with traumatic brain injuries, paralysis, and other disabilities that limit mobility, speech and hearing. Some exist now, or are in pilot phases, including new iterations of programs designed to help students with reading disabilities such as dyslexia and dysgraphia, auditory challenges, and vision impairment. There are also technologies that use motion capture to convert American Sign Language into speech and text for students who are deaf or hard of hearing. Machine learning can also assist language learners who have relocated to a new country where they don't yet know the language.

GETTING STARTED WITH AI IN THE CLASSROOM

Explore the resources below, most of which are free and available to use with your students.

Microsoft Learning Tools and Immersive Reader have a wide variety of applications, from learning to read for the first time to supporting struggling readers. Learning Tools allows users of OneNote to highlight text, change the spacing between words and lettering, change contrasts and colors, identify syllables, identify and label parts of speech, and read in other languages. Enhanced dictation improves authoring text. Focus Mode supports sustained attention and improves reading speeds. Immersive Reader can read aloud from a mobile device, which is beneficial for visually impaired learners, and can also be used to help learners proofread their writing and learn basic grammar. Find out more by exploring this link: **onenote.com/learningtools**.

Microsoft Translator uses natural language processing to break the language barrier. You can speak or type in your own language to communicate with other participants, and they will see your message in their own language. The Translator add-in for Outlook allows users to read and translate emails in their preferred language. Presentation Translator, a Microsoft Garage project, breaks down the language barrier by allowing users to offer live, subtitled presentations straight from PowerPoint. As they speak, the add-in is powered by the Microsoft Translator live feature, allowing the user to display subtitles directly onto PowerPoint presentations in any one of more than 60 supported text languages. This feature can also be used for audiences who are deaf or hard of hearing. Additionally, up to

100 audience members in the same room can follow along with the presentation in their own language on their phone, tablet, or computer. Explore more at: **translator.microsoft.com**.

Motion Savvy has UNI, a two-way communication software, in pilot phases now. UNI utilizes a camera to track the location of both hands and all ten fingers, translating American Sign Language into speech and text. There is live feedback and a graphic representation of the hands in order to make sure gestures are correctly captured. The user can add customized signs, as the software's dictionary can be expanded and uploaded to the internet to share with others. The more an individual uses the system, the more accurate the machine learning becomes. The system includes Dragon Nuance Pro, one of the leading pieces of voice recognition software. Watch the video and learn more at: **motionsavvy.com**.

Read Robert Szczerba's "Four Game-Changing Technologies for the Deaf and Hard of Hearing": **tinyurl.com/y89f7kyv**.

As we've seen in this chapter, AI development needs more work to progress from theory to reality. To reach beyond machine learning's limitations, scientists need to know more about the way the human brain works (Bransford & Schwartz, 1999).

An article published in *The Verge* in 2018 says, "Raw computing power isn't the be-all and end-all for AI success. Ingenuity in how you design your algorithms counts for at least as much" (Vincent, 2018). The article points out that in an AI engineering challenge in which large tech companies such as Google and Intel competed against smaller teams from universities and government departments, the top three teams that produced the fastest and cheapest algorithms all consisted of student researchers connected with Fast.AI, a nonprofit group dedicated to making deep learning "accessible to all." The institute's co-founder attributed his students' success to their ability to think creatively, which enabled them to produce winning results using basic resources. He wants people to know that anyone can do great things using accessible resources.

UNDERSTANDING AI

Read the article on how an AI speed test shows clever coders can still beat tech giants like Google and Intel: **tinyurl.com/y8d8pfdh**.

Ethical Considerations

Although the final chapter of this book will explore the ethical considerations of AI in greater detail, it is important to think about them early and often. As we've seen, an algorithm and its ability to accurately predict or infer is only as good as its training data—and how that data is collected makes a difference. Much of the data that is currently being collected comes from research institutions and medical institutions, whose data samples may be inherently biased and may not provide a full, accurate picture for inference and prediction. Companies are also collecting massive amounts of data on all of us all the time through our use of the internet, mobile devices, and computers.

To build a reasonable model, Jared Zimmerman says, one needs a minimum of 10,000 labeled sets—and even with that, the model will not be completely accurate. To be reasonably accurate, one needs around a million labeled data points. Big data companies need a lot of data from us to be able to create accurate models. Because the technology has developed so rapidly, laws and protocols have not yet clearly defined which data can be accessed freely, and for what purposes.

With AI still in its infancy, inaccurate or biased models can lead to unintended consequences, as Nathan Laurie and Nile Wilson have pointed out. So can AI that achieves a goal entirely through its own thinking, prompting Major Shelhorse to emphasize the importance of maintaining human control of machine learning—to not let it go entirely on its own.

Another ethical consideration surrounds the questions posed in the film, *Humans Need Not Apply* (**youtu.be/7Pq-S557XQU**). Automation and the resulting job shifts could lead to displacement of employees who have developed only one skill set and are unable to adapt when their jobs become replaceable by a machine. In that case, the burden is on us as educators to determine proactive measures to support our young people as they learn how to prepare for a world in which machine learning becomes increasingly refined and ubiquitous.

When asked what he wants teachers to know about a future with AI, Jared Zimmerman says that students should learn statistics and programming concepts. Designers of artificial intelligence and machine learning must move from designing prescriptively to designing descriptively. In other words, instead of telling systems how to do things, you teach a goal and see how it gets there. He described it as similar to teaching children: They might surprise you and think of a process you never would have imagined (J. Zimmerman, personal communication, May 9, 2018).

ISTE Standards for Students and Teachers

Tying in the content from this chapter with the first chapter and the introduction, we should reexamine what we want young people to be able to do when they complete formal education. That task can be daunting, but it is helpful to know that the International Society for Technology in Education (ISTE) has provided a guideline in the form of the ISTE Standards for Students (**iste.org/standards/for-students**) to help anchor educators and provide direction. We know that technology will constantly evolve. That means we need to adapt with it—and teach our young people to be adaptable. The standards have been created to ensure that learners drive their own learning that their voice is heard and involved.

We need to be aware of what exists now, while also keeping an eye toward the future, so we can support and guide our young people. We also want students to be able to identify and discern verifiable claims, use the knowledge that they've gained, and transfer that learning to create something that will lead us closer to finding solutions to local and global challenges. Beyond knowledge, we want learners to persevere through difficult times and become resilient. Through that, we want them to learn compassion and empathy, so they can design creative solutions to people's problems. We want learners to have the ability to adapt and be flexible when learning new skills. We them to become responsible and develop their ability to work with others. We want them to learn from the past without becoming stuck in it, doomed to repeat documented failures. We want them to be discerning, so they aren't led to believe just anything.

In societies that value workplace skills that support innovation, there needs to be an alignment between the way young people learn and what we want them to be able to do as they become contributing members of society.

In some ways, what we want young people to be able to do at the end of their formal education is very different than the current capability of machines and the state of AI (Allen, 2011). There still exist aspects of learning that are uniquely human. To our knowledge, there exists no AI in practice that can transfer knowledge to a new domain in the same way a human can while making inferences and processing sensory information to create, innovate, and respond to a broad range of settings and scenarios. Currently, that level of AI remains in the domain of science fiction. And yet, seeing the capabilities of AI that exist around us now can give humans the inspiration to dream of what might be possible (Turbot, 2017; Kurshan, 2016).

REFLECTING ON AI ·

- Watch and discuss the film, *Humans Need Not Apply* (**youtu.be/7Pq-S557XQU**). What surprised you about the capabilities machines already have?

- What are some things machines still can't do as well as humans?

- What jobs do you and your learners imagine will exist in the future if today's jobs become automated?

- How is human learning similar to the way a machine learns? How do humans and machines learn differently?

- What are some initial ethical concerns that should be considered?

· ·

To understand how AI works, educators and students alike first need to develop a firm grasp of both its capabilities and its limitations. Keep your answers to these questions in mind as you explore different approaches to teaching with AI in the next chapter.

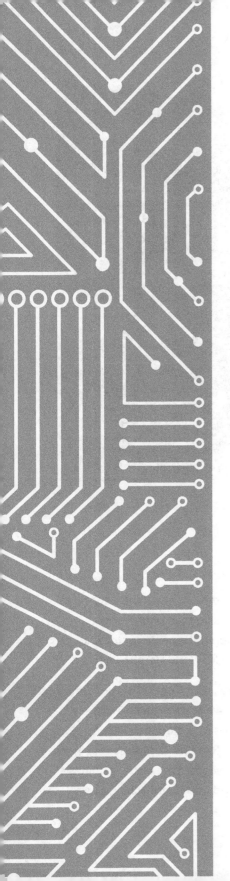

CHAPTER 3
Approaches to Teaching with AI

Way of Tea and Design Thinking

DRAMATIS PERSONAE

HIDEKAZU SHOTO: Head of ICT Department and English teacher at Ritsumeikan Primary School

MIKI HORIE, PHD: Principal of Ritsumeikan Primary School and associate professor at Ritsumeikan University

MICHELLE ZIMMERMAN: Author and educator

SCENE

Dr. Miki Horie and Hidekazu Shoto are giving the author a tour of Ritsumeikan Primary School in Kyoto, Japan.

TIME: October, 2017

Figure 3.1   Kyoto, Japan, October 2017.

ACT I

Scene 3

SETTING: In Kyoto, the centuries-old former capital of Japan, the leaves on the trees have begun to turn shades of gold and red. In a month, they'll achieve their peak hues of vibrant garnets, ruby reds, and oranges. Kyoto is still considered the center of tradition and culture in Japan, with many historic buildings and UNESCO World Heritage sites.

There are eleven wards in the city of Kyoto. Kita (北区 *Kita-ku*), is one of them. The name means "North Ward." Ritsumeikan Primary School is a short walk from Kitaōji Train Station (北大路駅 *Kitaōji-eki*) in Kita-Ku. The primary school is affiliated with Ritsumeikan University (立命館大学 *Ritsumeikan Daigaku*, abbreviated to Rits and 立命 *Ritsumei*) in Kyoto. This private university, founded in 1869, derives its name from the ancient Chinese philosopher Mencius, who spoke about cultivating one's mind and "establishing one's destiny" (in Japanese, 立命, *ritsumei*). The "kan" added to the end represents a place. So the name "Ritsumeikan" means "the place to establish one's destiny."

Ritsumeikan University is considered one of western Japan's four leading private universities. Well-known for its international relations program, it has exchange programs throughout the world including with the University of British Columbia, the University of Melbourne, the University of Sydney, the University of Hong Kong, and King's College London. The primary school's motto is "Raising children to be global-minded," indicating a school community that cultivates ethics and open-mindedness and values every child's individuality.

AT RISE:

心のコップを上にしよう

An upside down cup
Cannot be filled, a value
Preserved tradition

Figure 3.2 Tea bowls made by students at Ritsumeikan Primary.

In a quiet hall with glistening hardwood floors, a row of dark pottery lines a light-colored shelf against a wall. The glaze, called *Kuro-yu*, both balances and contrasts with the surfaces and textures in the space: the smooth, straight lines of the shelves and floor planks versus the pottery's circular forms—each unique, varying in size, shape, depth, and different levels of gloss. This pottery is proudly displayed, each vessel open, waiting to be filled with the mixture of life-giving water and tradition encapsulated by matcha tea, a finely ground powder made from green tea leaves grown in the shade and dissolved in liquid.

The pieces of pottery lining the wall are tea bowls, part of the tea equipment called *chadōgu*, created by children from the ages of 10 to 12 years old in preparation for learning Way of Tea at Ritsumeikan Primary. In Japanese, the tea ceremony is called *chanoyu* (or *sadō* or *chadō*) and is considered one of the three classical arts of refinement. The Way of Tea encompasses several principles: harmony (*wa*), respect (*kei*), purity (*sei*), and tranquility (*jaku*). It is not just about tea; it is an event that honors relationship, supported by a philosophy that each gathering should be valued because that moment in time is unique and can never be replicated. All of this is part of the ethical studies learners' experience as they plumb the deeper meaning and importance of life, living, and human relationships as part of their "Ritsumei Studies." One goal is to create a space where children learn human interaction and how to respect the value of ethical behavior and self-discipline. The traditional Japanese-style room allows children to learn etiquette and develop manners while becoming part of the Way of Tea and learning the art of arranging flowers, known as *Kadō* ("way of flowers").

Figure 3.3
Student robotics projects in progress at Ritsumeikan Primary School, Kyoto, Japan.

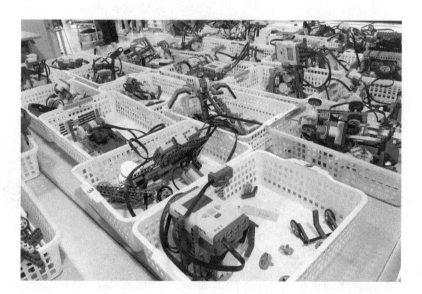

Around the corner, a room full of plastic bins contains student robotics projects in progress. Behind glass doors leading to the adjacent room, young children smile, giggle, and bubble with effervescence as they edit video projects that show their robotics designs, reflect on what worked and what failed, and explain their process in English. They combine world language skills with design thinking and STEM learning as they collaborate and create media artifacts to communicate their learning to an audience outside of their school.

We continue down another hall, with high-gloss hardwood floors and a row of sinks on one side. At the end of the hall, a robot stands near a gray container corralling umbrellas with lime green handles.

Figure 3.4
A hall at Ritsumeikan Primary School, Kyoto, Japan.

We turn into another learning space, where children are using Minecraft Education Edition to replicate the sights they saw during a visit to Kyoto's local World Heritage sites. They work collaboratively to create representations of their city inside a Minecraft world for other people in different locations to explore.

Figure 3.5
Students at Ritsumeikan Primary School use Minecraft Educational Edition to replicate World Heritage sites they have visited in Kyoto.

At the end of the day, the students maintain their smiles as they clean their environment—not just the desks and tables, but the floors as well. There's a reason the hallways gleam. There is more to that row of dark glazed pottery lining the light-colored shelf in a quiet hall with glistening hardwood floors.

End Scene 3

GOING DEEPER WITH VIDEOS ·

Watch, think, and dig deeper with the TED-Ed video on the History of Tea: **ed.ted.com/lessons/the-history-of-tea-shunan-teng**.

Listen to Ritsumeikan Primary students talk about keeping their school clean—a task they share as they learn to become stewards of their environment. Contrast this philosophy with the Pixar movie *WALL-E*, which shows what happens when humans don't learn to take care of their own community: **youtu.be/jv4oNvxCY5k**.

· ·

REFLECTING ON AI ·

- What does the description above have to do with a discussion on approaches to teaching AI?

- Why do you think tea was used to introduce this chapter and not the modern technology the school is using?

- In previous chapters, the amount of text for the "setting" was less and the "at rise" of the action was more. Why do you think the description above includes a longer setting?

- Why was the first line of the "at rise" section written in Japanese?

- If you don't know how to speak or read Japanese, what are some ways of decoding those characters to understand the meaning?

- What was the purpose of setting the stage with the message in the haiku? What do you think the poem means?

- Haiku poetry follows a specific pattern. What is the value in limiting poetic expression to a specific number of lines and syllables?

- In literary terms, foreshadowing is an indication of a future event. How do you think the haiku could be foreshadowing what is coming in this chapter and what it has to do with AI?

- What is something from Chapter 1 or Chapter 2 that you can connect to this story?

- What is the value of storytelling?

- How do the school's name, Ritsumeikan, and the concepts embodied in the Way of Tea provide a lens for thinking about the learning that educators need as we approach AI?

- What does Ritsumeikan Primary want its students to be able to do at the end of their formal education?

- What does "raising children to be global-minded" mean to you?

- In Japanese culture, contrasts serve a valuable purpose. What are some of the contrasts you noticed in the introduction, and how can contrasts be beneficial in an investigation of AI?

- In what ways did Ritsumeikan Primary's use of technology surprise you?

- Why do learners help keep their school clean? How do they benefit from this?

- What subject matter domains does the school combine?

- What tools did students use to demonstrate their learning?

- What could the video about students learning to keep their environment clean have to do with a discussion on approaches to teaching for a world with AI?

Integrating AI into Existing Curriculum

Almost 20 years into the new millennium, informally known as the digital age, ancient practices such as the Japanese tea ceremony may seem out of place among the rapidly advancing technologies students use today. How can the Way of Tea help prepare students to "thrive in a constantly evolving technological landscape" (ISTE, 2018)? As Ritsumeikan Primary students explore these questions themselves, they learn to make connections between different concepts. Like a tea bowl waiting to be filled—or a machine-learning algorithm ready for training data—their receptiveness to new ideas enables them to learn. Unlike AI, they are then able to transfer their learning across domains as they switch seamlessly between pouring tea, editing videos, and cleaning their school.

This flexibility of thought is an absolute necessity in an age of accelerating change. The more time passes, the faster technology advances. Nicole Krueger reports in a recent ISTE blog post that "the overall share of jobs requiring AI skills has grown 4.5 times in the past five years, and it will only continue to climb as the technology becomes more widespread" (Krueger, 2018). As educators, the onus is on us to keep up and to support our students, no matter what subject area, so it becomes second nature for them to use established and emerging technologies to support their learning and their work. Your K-12 students were born into the digital age. As technology advances, teachers must advance with it, and this can be overwhelming. Krueger suggests that "as with any technology, the key to integrating AI successfully is to start with the learning goal, and then ask how AI can help students get there" (Krueger, 2018).

We have numerous learning goals in every subject area. With the integration of new technologies, there are additional goals we must model to help students become:

EMPOWERED LEARNERS who leverage technology to take an active role in choosing, achieving, and demonstrating competency toward their learning goals, informed by the learning sciences.

DIGITAL CITIZENS who recognize the rights, responsibilities, and opportunities of living, learning, and working in an interconnected digital world, and who act in ways that are safe, legal, and ethical.

KNOWLEDGE CONSTRUCTORS who critically curate a variety of resources using digital tools to construct knowledge, produce creative artifacts, and create meaningful learning experiences for themselves and others.

CREATIVE COMMUNICATORS who develop and employ strategies for understanding and solving problems in ways that leverage the power of technological methods to develop and test solutions.

GLOBAL COLLABORATORS who use digital tools to broaden their perspectives and enrich their learning by collaborating with others and working effectively in teams locally and globally.

In the previous chapter, we looked at businesses and fields where AI is already in use and addressed the importance of preparing students for the future job market. In the digital age, this this is increasingly becoming a priority in the K-12 classroom. Unlike the agricultural age or the industrial age, the tools and applications of the digital age will be ubiquitous in the job markets of the future.

While classroom teachers today are often overwhelmed with mandated curriculum content and related standards, it has also become our job to prepare students for an ever-evolving, technology-rich workplace, and to be aware that higher education students are expected to be proficient in emerging technologies. In their article "The Benefit of Integrating Technology into the Classroom," Ranasinghe and Leisher (2009) assert that "part of the responsibility of educators, both at the high school and college level, is to prepare students for entering the job market" (p. 3). They further suggest that "integrating technology into the classroom begins with the teacher preparing lessons that use technology in meaningful and relevant ways, using technology to support curriculum rather than dominate it" (p. 4).

In this chapter, we will examine ways AI can support instruction in the STEM and STEAM fields, as well as project-based learning, design thinking, and storytelling. We'll review related ISTE standards and take a look at Next Generation Science Standards (NGSS). By modeling the application of AI, you are helping students become familiar with AI and grow accustomed to using it as a tool in their work.

Applying What We Know about AI to Education

While there is an ongoing debate about what counts as human intelligence, we might also consider that there will be a debate about what counts as an intelligent machine. In the first two chapters, we looked at ways people talk about AI. We looked at how machine learning—a subfield of AI—works. At the time of this book's publication, no one has yet figured out how to create true AI. As with many topics, the more one learns, the more one realizes how much more there is to learn. You may recall from Chapter 1 that in 1955, a group of ambitious professors from Dartmouth believed it was possible to solve the challenge of AI over a summer. The challenge proved more complex than they imagined. While there have been many predictions since the earliest research in AI was conducted, further unanticipated challenges have emerged. In Paul Allen's article "The Singularity Isn't Near," he shares that "as we learn more about the brain we see a greater degree of neural variation and it's getting harder the more we learn. That means there's more work that needs to be done in understanding how human intelligence works before we can get machines to replicate it" (Allen, 2011).

One of the challenges for us, as educators, is to understand the questions: If AI is still theoretical, how can we apply it in the classroom or develop approaches to teaching

AI? What are we actually teaching or preparing students for? Teaching them how to code and create chatbots is good, but what happens when AI can pump out basic code faster than a human can? Unless we show students how to leverage the human aspects of their learning—curiosity, creativity, making connections—we end up teaching them to think like a machine that only follows a set of procedures. The following are some considerations when teaching and learning with AI.

AI LANGUAGE AND VOCABULARY

It can be challenging to think of instructional approaches when there are so many different ways of thinking about AI. This book has already presented a variety of reflection questions, media to watch, and links to further reading on AI. As you have read, people are using these technologies in a variety of fields and occupations, from the arts and animation to material sciences and healthcare. In areas of new knowledge that cross multiple domains or draw on various research traditions to create foundations for work, it is common for some language and vocabulary to come across as muddled, sometimes blurring together, making it difficult to grasp. Searching a multitude of resources produces some overlap and variation in how people define aspects of AI or use different language when talking about the same technology.

FLEXIBILITY

As humans, we have the capacity to learn to be adaptable, flexible, and fluid in our movements, thoughts, and processes. Being a teacher in the digital age means being flexible—able to adapt to change. In its current state, AI can only solve certain problems; machines can't do what we do in terms of adaptability. For example, our flexibility allows us to notice wires out of place that may be interfering with a robot trying to assemble something in an industrial plant (Akella, 2018). The human can easily brush the wires to the side to allow the assembly to continue. However, a machine would not only have difficulty recognizing the wires, it would have a problem moving the wires out of the way.

For now, we can only imagine what lies ahead. As the digital age unfolds, the education system and its teachers must be flexible and able to adapt to change. In the digital age, a teacher's role may change as AI is incorporated, but we will always be needed and can never be replaced, as some have worried.

ETHICS

If we are to interact with machines that are designed to replicate human intelligence, how will we learn from them—and them from us? How might that change who we are as humans—and who they are as machines? We assume that ethics emerge from necessity through sociocultural interactions and influences. If, for example, you were the only person in the world, would you need to develop ethics, knowing your actions or behaviors or thoughts had no chance of impacting another living being? In a space with other intelligent beings, how do we deal with each other at a social level, at a national level, or at a global level? This prompts the question: How do we approach preparing students for the new frontiers moving toward AI, and have we established a set of ethics as part of that process?

CULTURE

We bring our own biases and cultural norms into the design of cognitive systems that power robotics and machine learning. When classes of children, ages five, six, and seven, were asked what they wished robots could do, and how they would design their robot, many of those children chose tasks that they or their parents did not want to do. These included picking up the trash, washing the dishes, cleaning their room, and completing their homework. Recall from the first chapter the description of the origins of the word "robot." Recall also the Disney Pixar film *WALL-E*, a cautionary story about what happens when humans choose not to take responsibility for their surroundings and rely on machines to do everything they don't want to do for themselves. This animated story shows the negative impact that mindset can have on both humanity and the planet. Like an upside-down cup that cannot be filled, disconnecting from our environment cuts off our ability to learn from it. Ritsumeikan Primary School in Kyoto, Japan attempts to ward off this potential dystopian future by cultivating a culture of stewardship among its students, who take responsibility for their environment rather than looking to machines to do it for them.

The cultural implications of AI make it vital that culture remains a part of the process as schools lay the foundation for students to effectively interact with new technologies while engaging in project-based learning, STEM, and design thinking. The key to retaining the uniqueness of schools around the world is to not abandon each school's rich heritage for the sake of modern technology. We should maintain a mission within our individual schools and the communities they serve to ensure they have a clearly defined culture, allowing history to be restored, renewed, and maintained in order to not forget the past. By adapting our vision for the future, we can demonstrate a synthesis of existing culture and machine learning. An example of this is the Ritsumeikan Primary students creating a representation of World Heritage sites in Minecraft Education Edition, as seen in their YouTube video (**youtu.be/FII6bQzRsow**) and in Figure 3.5 in the opening scene to this chapter.

In this school, educators have acknowledged how gaming motivates students. They have chosen to harness that motivation and challenge students to determine ways to represent local historic sites that are part of their culture through the game. Read more about the intercultural Minecraft project between Ritsumeikan Primary in Kyoto Japan, and Renton Prep in Renton, Washington: **rentonprep.org/ intercultural-minecraft-project**.

REFLECTING ON AI

- If artificial general intelligence is created, will it deviate from the culture it was originally programmed with, will it learn from the culture within which it operates, or will it create its own culture? How so?

- If AI develops its own culture, what might sociocultural interactions look like as humans interact with machines?

- What kind of future environment and culture do we want to live in, locally and globally?

Teaching Within a Rapidly Advancing Field

Rapid advances in AI make it challenging for educators to determine a teaching approach and pin down relevant information that will persist through the ongoing changes, especially when those in the field are collaborating with a wide variety of content experts who may talk about AI differently. New articles come out daily. While participating in professional development sessions and educational technology conferences, we may hope to stumble upon a single clear path—a set of tools or a checklist that can simplify teaching with this new technology. Our thinking may resonate with sentiments such as: "Great, another tool I have to learn," or, "How can I add this into my already packed schedule?" or, "There is so much information out there, how can I sort through it all?"

Questions about what is still theoretical at this point—and what is already in use in practical settings—can raise more questions about how we can prepare students for the new frontier with AI. You may ask yourself: What does it all mean, and how does it work? It is okay if your thinking shifts on your journey as you explore approaches to teaching on this new frontier. As the field advances, ideas will grow and shift. New knowledge will challenge old assumptions. Debates will continue. Definitions will morph, as there is still no single, clearly articulated definition that all agree upon for artificial intelligence. New frontiers can be messy and ambiguous places, but that is part of the excitement. As Juli Lorton, one of my research methods instructors at University of Washington, said, "It just means the area is ripe for research." She added, "That's the time to explore and blaze trails, not turn to a well-traveled path" (J. Lorton, personal communication, 2018).

Preparing students for a future with AI demands more than teaching word processing, media presentation, or coding language, because there are so many facets to consider as humans increasingly interact with machines. This means there is not one single program or course of action we can point to as a successful implementation of a single AI curriculum, or of teaching with AI as a tool. But the good news is that there are things you can do now with your students that will persist while the tools and technology continue to change around you. As one physics professor from California Polytechnic State University, San Luis Obispo, said, "If a machine can replace a teacher, it should" (personal communication, 2018).

What he meant by that is, as educators, we should not replicate what a machine is capable of, such as rote memory, inflexible lessons, standardized grading, basic skills, and established facts. Machines will never tire of seeing an incorrect answer for 2+2 over and over, or seeing the same word misspelled multiple times. Students also take correction from a machine less personally than when it comes from a human educator. For the more tedious tasks, machines can, for example, harness gamification to increase student motivation to practice those skills. That frees educators to find ways to harness what they excel at as humans, such as developing effective questioning strategies; transferring learning from one setting to another; and constructing knowledge.

Kai-Fu Lee, a venture capitalist from Taiwan, has worked in AI for more than 30 years and opened Google's China office. He has said AI isn't capable of empathy and that "we have a human responsibility" to develop and apply empathy. The other things he said AI cannot do well include creativity, dexterity, and complexity (Anderson (1), 2018).

"High-Touch and High-Tech" Learning

The former minister of education, science, and technology in South Korea, Ju Ho Lee, is now professor at the KDI School of Public Policy and Management. He said in a recent article (Anderson (2), 2018) that "high-touch, high-tech" learning—where high-touch is learning that is more project-based and done with the support of teachers, and high-tech is adaptive learning supported by AI and mobile devices—is the only direction for the future. This model is based on the well-established Bloom's Taxonomy. The article includes an illustration of the model, from Dale Johnson, adaptive program manager at Arizona State University. The model demonstrates the foundation that needs to be in place before students can create, becoming empowered learners, knowledge constructors, and innovative designers. Since machines are excellent at remembering, they should support the knowledge and content acquisition at the base of the model. Contrary to some popular opinion, it is still beneficial for students to memorize some basic content knowledge.

To efficiently comprehend text, students need to know what words mean and how to say them. Without some automaticity from memorization, it becomes difficult to comprehend the meaning of a story because the amount of work it takes to decode information and hold it in short-term memory is too much for the brain to process all at once (Baddeley, 1998) while also comprehending the story. Memorizing phonics sounds can help emergent readers with the decoding process for words they don't yet remember. Medina states it simply, "We repeat to remember" (2008). AI can help students understand and comprehend by reading words out loud using natural language processing. This reduces the cognitive load, so students don't need to use valuable cognitive resources in stopping to decode each word that is not yet in long-term memory. When students fill up their short-term memory trying to decode each word, they are not able to hold the information long enough to recall all of the words and process what they mean together. The continuity is lost by trying to figure out each word.

As we determine approaches to preparing for a world with AI, we must continually ask ourselves what we want young people to be able to do when they complete formal education. What do we want our society or world to become? There must be a vision, a mission, a problem to solve, and an action. While attending the Disney Institute for Business Excellence in the summer of 2016, I learned that Disney continues to adapt its vision for the future while maintaining the same mission. Without the ability to continually adapt to new advancements, Disney wouldn't stay relevant. And yet, the Disney brand remains consistent in its mission, so we can recognize and connect to it. As we prepare students for these new frontiers with emerging elements of AI, we need to prepare them to thrive in a place where change is constant and ambiguity abounds. We need them to know that new headlines in the media today may be different in 5 or 10 years. Do you recall the discussion in Chapter 1 on AI winters? Headlines and overpromises of AI's capabilities led to disillusionment and decreased funding. New knowledge led to new challenges that evoked to feelings of failure and defeat.

How, then, do we prepare young people for careers in the medical field or technology-based professions that involve mathematics, statistical analysis, and the ability to collaborate in groups to find solutions to problems that will advance these fields? Two approaches include design thinking and STEM.

Design Thinking

Innovators in creative fields ranging from literature to engineering use an iterative process known as **design thinking** to experiment, test out ideas, and refine their approach. By learning this process, students can use it to address any problem they encounter. It begins with learning to empathize, then defining the problem, ideating, and prototyping, followed by a period of testing, feedback, and reflection. A classroom that uses design thinking is a highly structured environment that fosters creativity.

UNDERSTANDING AI

- Watch the Design Thinking Teacher Training video: **youtu.be/qqM8If3zfFo**.
- Investigate the Stanford website of the Hasso Plattner Institute of Design at Stanford (d.school) to learn more about design thinking: **dschool.stanford.edu**.
- The Global Day of Design (**globaldayofdesign.com**) focuses on using the design thinking process in school. The goal is to inspire a transformation in schools around the world to incorporate design into their everyday practice with students. In the past two years, more than 100,000 students from 950 schools on four continents have participated (Global Day of Design, 2018).

DIVERGENT THINKING FOR DESIGN

People aren't inherently left-brained or right-brained. The human mind is capable of developing the ability to make connections work around constraints to come up with new solutions. One of our jobs as educators should include an approach to learning that helps young people practice expanding their brain's capabilities. Briggs (2014) pointed out that decades of research have shown that when students are exposed to divergent thinking methods early in their education, they become more creative—both immediately and later on as adults.

UNDERSTANDING AI ·

Watch the PBS documentary *Between the Folds* (**pbs.org/independentlens/between-the-folds/film.html**), and discuss the divergent thinking seen in the documentary and how the arts and sciences can inform each other. What are some examples of creative constraints?

Extended project: Use creative constraints for storytelling. A good example of this is Renton Prep middle school student Jennifer Fernandez's film that combines a study of Japan with folk tales, illustrated with origami: **youtube.com/watch?v=VfT2IQ3hISI**.

· ·

Making connections and speaking fluidly are two things humans do well that machines cannot. In an article for UploadVR titled "AI and Storytelling: An Unlikely Friendship," Rob Ogden talked about what AI could do for the future of storytelling as it merges with visual imagery and gaming:

> *AI can breathe life into the infinite worlds that will make VR the truly immersive alternate universe that it can and should be. It can populate those worlds with realistic and compelling characters that can be enjoyed whether someone is playing by themselves or within a massively multiplayer setting (Ogden, 2017).*

To explore visual imagery and learn to communicate ideas creatively, we need to start with basics.

LEARNING WITH PAPER AND A SQUIGGLE ·

One approach to helping students with divergent thinking is inspired by a 1978 book called the *Anti-Coloring Book* by Susan Striker. The image can be found online here: **tiny.cc/iif7wy**.

Students: All ages. I have done this activity with educators in training as well as students.

Supplies: Have a surface and something with which to leave a mark. This could be dirt and a stick. It could be a piece of paper and a pencil.

Helpful hint: By standardizing the squiggle or curve, you can help all students see how many variations can exist.

PROCESS:
First Method (or First Iteration of the Design)

1. Create a squiggle or use the image in the link above.

2. Read together or have students read the prompt: "A famous artist needs your help. The artist started this picture but was stung on the thumb by a bee. Turn the picture any way you'd like and finish it."

3. Give students complete freedom with no other instructions.

4. Display completed images and have a discussion on the similarities and differences they see among the completed images.

5. Ask questions like:

    a. What are examples that surprised you or are unexpected?

    b. What are examples that are closer to what you expected to see?

    c. If you had a chance to do this again, what would you do differently?

6. You may choose to end the activity here, or you can go for a second round.

Second Method (or Second Iteration of the Design)

1. Create a squiggle or use the image in the link above.

2. Hold it up or replicate the image on an enlarged surface for the class to see. This could be hand-drawn on poster paper or a black/white/smart board, a projection from a device with digital ink to a screen, or in virtual or mixed reality.

3. Start a discussion to ask students to quickly identify what the squiggle reminds them of or what it looks like.

4. Explain that the goal is to create an image or design that disguises the curve so someone who never saw initial drawing wouldn't know it was already there on this page. This establishes a first constraint.

5. Explain what a creative constraint is and watch the TED-Ed video on the Power of Creative Constraints: **ed.ted.com/lessons/the-power-of-creative-constraints-brandon-rodriguez**.

6. Write a collaborative list of ideas. (Some common ideas might include river, mountains, clouds, puddle, etc.).

7. Rotate the page to a new orientation from portrait (vertical) to landscape (horizontal) and see if new ideas come up by seeing the curve from another perspective. Add those to the collaborative list so all students can see.

8. Ask the students if it is acceptable to turn the paper on a diagonal. (The answer is "yes" as the purpose is to break students from the expected norms of how paper is oriented, while the direction and shape of the curve remains constant.)

9. Explain that by keeping the curve the same for everyone (copy of the original image) there are two things happening: 1) It is something that is held constant. 2) It introduces a second constraint that cannot be altered.

10. Ask the students if they can come up with any more ideas for how they can complete the curve, and add those to the collaborative list.

11. If students are new to practicing becoming innovative designers and creative communicators you may stop there and let them choose an idea from the list to execute based on those two constraints only. Finish with the reflective discussion from the First Method. If this is their second iteration, move on to the Third Method.

Third Method (or Third Iteration of the Design, Advanced)

1. Follow the procedure for suggested steps 1–11 for the Second Method.

2. Once the collaborative list of ideas has reached a point where no one else can think of any possibilities, draw a big "X" through the entire list and, depending on the humor level of your class and your relationship with them, or the culture of the class, you can say simply, "Outlawed."

3. Once students get over the initial shock, gasps, and complaints that there are no other possible ways you can complete the image if those ideas aren't allowed, you explain further. All those ideas have already been generated. They are good ideas. All of them would make great images. How do we know?

Because they are expected and relatively easy to imagine. How do we know? Because all of you came up with the great ideas already. But why are they outlawed? Why won't I let any of you use those ideas? Because I want you to come up with something *unexpected*. I want you to challenge yourself to think of something that no one in this class has ever thought of before.

4. Ask students to sketch three to five possible ideas as small thumbnail images and come back the next day to show them to classmates.

5. When students show the quick sketches to classmates, have them ask: "Which one do you think is the most unexpected? Why do you say that?"

6. Let students decide which sketch they want to pursue based on feedback.

7. Discuss this process in class and ask if any students came up with the same idea as anyone else. Then say that no two images can be exactly alike. Challenge students to think of a new approach to make theirs unexpected and unlike anyone else's design. If there is a dispute over who came up with the idea first, you can have students practice ways to resolve the dispute or help each other come up with a new iteration that provides enough variation so the two concepts don't look identical.

8. Have students draft a design based on their chosen concept and display all of the images around the room.

9. Conduct a gallery walk in silence. As students walk around the room and look at all of the designs, ask them to look for things that catch their attention or surprise them.

10. Have a debrief with the class and ask them to point out what caught their attention or surprised them and why. This is helping students practice providing critique in a positive way first, as well as practice communicating and collaborating.

11. Ask students what sparked ideas they wouldn't have thought of on their own, and whether there is something they would redesign if given the opportunity.

12. Ask students which designs most effectively disguised the curve by incorporating it into their design so thoroughly that it appears there was no original curve on the page. Discuss what makes this possible. (It may include using a dark pen to continue the curve or changing the thickness of lines.)

13. Give students a chance to re-draft their designs based on feedback and incorporate what they learned from the gallery walk.

14. As a final draft constraint, consider having students look at aesthetics and boldness by stepping back and viewing their image from a distance. Ask students what catches their eye and stands out at a distance and why. It may be bold colors, bold shapes, placement of the image, or a very unexpected design. Ask them to determine what they need to do to make their design stand out in the final version.

I conducted this process multiple times with her students and varied the time constraint, the materials constraint (pen only, colors, different media allowed, and scanning to create with digital ink). One student asked if the class could add an additional constraint as it was December, and the class voted to require a winter or Christmas-inspired theme. The class started the Third Method process again by coming up with a winter-themed collaborative list and then outlawing it. Several students found loopholes and had fun pushing the boundaries of the challenge. Watch the video to see their final designs for ages 11-15: **youtu.be/skUtiU5YYoE**.

VISUAL THINKING: STRATEGIES TO SUPPORT DESIGN THINKING IN MACHINE LEARNING

Whether you consider yourself an artist or not, you can use resources that are already created and accessible to teachers to help you as you guide your students in visual thinking strategies (VTS) that support STEM, STEAM, and design thinking.

Explore VTS for developing close looking, flexible thinking, careful listening, and collaboration. VTS does not require the use of computers, but it can include image searches. Start by accessing images that can be found in magazines, photography, textbooks, children's picture books, or advertisements. VTS is based on three primary questions to begin discussions with students based on images:

1. What is going on in this picture?
2. What do you see that makes you say that?
3. What more can we find?

VTS can support students as they build connections. Read more about visual thinking research and theory at **vtshome.org**.

What does all this have to do with approaches to teaching AI? Recall that for AI to work, machines need to take in a lot of information. One of those types of information is visual information, called **computer vision**. Digital photography using a phone or camera isn't the same as computer vision. For about 50 years, computer scientists have been trying to help computers understand imagery. That has led to the ability of computers to track hands and whole bodies; of biometrics to unlock phones and computer screens; of facial recognition software such as the technology China is now using to track people on the streets (Anwar, 2018) and in classrooms (Chan, 2018); and of autonomous vehicles to understand their surroundings (Crash Course, 2017).

Computer vision is helping to break language barriers. Language translators can now take an image of typed characters and, with computer vision to natural language processing, the program can translate the language.

TRANSLATION AND VISIBILE THINKING ·

Download the Microsoft Translator app (**translator.microsoft.com**) and use it to translate the line of Japanese in the "At Rise" section of this chapter's opening scene into English (or another language). Compare that to the English haiku beneath it. What do you think it means? How can a tea bowl be a symbol for an approach to teaching AI? Explore other translation options, including letting the translator create live captions on a Power Point presentation as one speaks the presentation. It can either be in the same language for accessibility, or in a different language. Through this process the presenter is becoming a creative communicator and global collaborator.

Check out this example of student work based on a field trip to the Seattle Art Museum, which incorporates culture, art, history, technology, and visual thinking strategies: **sway.office.com/5LKP2LhyoDfVO4pd**.

See how students combined arts, culture, history, tradition research, and AI to produce gifts for Japanese Diet (legislature) members and researchers who visited Renton Prep in September 2018. They documented their creative process and used AI tools to support their creative construction from documentation to communication, then used natural language processing (NLP) to help make their thinking visible to others in Japan. NLP is still developing and is not perfect; native Japanese speakers suggested the translation is about 70% accurate at this point: **sway.office.com/uox9YPUJ0mQx6Vwj**.

· ·

STEAM and the Arts

The National Science Foundation (NSF) has described aspects of the arts that support and are actually part of STEM learning, including "drawing on visual and graphical ideas, improvisation, narrative writing, and the process of using innovative visual displays of information for creating visual roadmaps" (Edger, 2017). It is also important to note that each area of STEM incorporates the arts in some way. John Maeda—president of the Rhode Island School of Design (RISD) from 2008-2013— has asserted that the arts (including liberal arts, fine arts, music, design thinking, and language arts) are critical components to innovation, and the artistic and design-related skills and thinking processes for student learning in STEM should be incorporated whenever appropriate (Gunn, 2017).

Design is but one example of how art comes into play when STEM subjects are addressed. Consider the work of a mechanical engineer, a physicist, or even a mathematician—the design arts are a parcel of what each of these professionals perform in the course of their work. In the *Edutopia* article "Full STEAM Ahead: Why Arts Are Essential in a STEM Education," Mary Beth Hertz writes:

> *Everyone from software engineers and aerospace technicians to biotechnical engineers, professional mathematicians, and laboratory scientists knows that building great things and solving real problems requires a measure of creativity. More and more, professional artists themselves are incorporating technological tools and scientific processes to their art." (Hertz, 2016)*

A growing number of educators are adding in the A for arts and turning STEM into STEAM. The inclusion of the arts also helps STEM professionals think creatively—to consider, for example, how experiments should be grounded in empathy and ethics.

We are told that people are either creative, artistic, and linguistic, or they are logical, mathematical, and scientific. A similar myth has been perpetuated that people are either right-brained or left-brained. In reality, both hemispheres of the brain are integrated. Neuroscientists know, and research has demonstrated, that math processing, for example, takes place in both hemispheres (Lombrozo, 2013).

John Medina's book *Brain Rules* (2008) showed that all brains are wired differently. Research shows that what you do and what you experience and learn in life physically changes what your brain looks like—literally rewiring it. Various regions of the brain develop at different rates and store information in different ways within different people. Additionally, research has shown that intelligence tests don't always show the many ways humans can display intelligence (p. 70). What does this mean for approaches to preparing students for a world with AI? It means that as we provide students with a range of experiences, their brains will develop pathways and practice making connections to come up with new ideas and questions.

Along with our knowledge of computer vision, the arts are an important part of a successful approach to preparing students for a future with AI. We saw how Pixar is using AI in animation, and can see more about how your students can learn STEAM with Pixar in a Box (**khanacademy.org/partner-content/pixar**).

Another application, Adobe Sensei, uses AI and ML for creative intelligence, or understanding the language of images, illustrations, and animations (**adobe.com/sensei. html**). Adobe Sensei, part of the Adobe Cloud Platform, searches and understands large amounts of content to help build workflow applications. What does this mean for the future? Image searches and working with imagery will become quicker and easier. But the software still doesn't create the content for you. The CEO of Adobe, Shantanu Narayen, is quoted on the Adobe Sensei website as saying, "Machine learning is going to change every single aspect of technology, but no machine will be able to mimic the creative ability of the human mind."

UNDERSTANDING AI ·

Read how Adobe Sensei is amplifying human creativity with artificial intelligence: **tinyurl.com/y72zqnuh**.

· ·

There is some debate as to whether machines will be able to fool humans into believing their creative products were created by another human. This has been explored through the use of AI to compose sonnets, haiku poetry, and music compositions. According to a TED-Ed talk, people have been wondering for generations if robots can be creative.

EXTENDED LEARNING ·

Watch the TED-Ed talk on Can Robots become Creative: **ed.ted.com/lessons/ can-robots-be-creative-gil-weinberg**.

Explore the Magenta blog to learn about Google's work with sketching and visual design: **magenta.tensorflow.org/sketch-rnn-demo**.

Make music and art using machine learning with Magenta: **magenta.tensorflow.org**.

Test your ability to determine if poetry is written by a machine or a human: **tinyurl.com/y9oubwuj**.

Explore how researchers in Japan are trying to create haiku from images using computer vision: **tinyurl.com/y8lskyxd**.

· ·

While machines excel at calculating mathematical possibilities—when beating humans at a game such as Go, for example—they have a harder time with the more subjective aspects of STEAM. In a 2018 article from the *Japan Times*, the authors say that "AI software has beaten top-ranking shogi and Go players by choosing what it sees as the best move out of the mathematical possibilities, but there is no absolute right or wrong in poetry, meaning it is difficult for the system to judge the quality of its work" (2018). According to Seattle Go Center instructor Mike Malveaux (M. Malveaux, personal communication, July 8, 2018), parables are part of the training when learning to play the game. While humans respond well to parables, machines do not. As a result, machines play the game differently than humans—in fact, some people are using AI to learn moves that aren't necessarily typical in the human repertoire. Although machines have become capable of beating humans at the game sooner than much of the Go community expected, some have failed miserably because they couldn't transfer strategies from one scenario to another, Malveaux said. As a result, the aesthetic elements of the game get lost.

Figure 3.6
Try playing Go against a machine: **playgo.to/iwtg/en/**

Teaching with AI in the Context of STEM Learning

Although scientists may agree on a process for the scientific method, experts have determined that learning science, in isolation from technology, engineering, and mathematics, is not fully preparing students for careers in which they'll need to combine these subjects to innovate and succeed. Combining science, technology, engineering, and mathematics in a meaningful way that allows students to apply their learning is referred to as STEM. STEM subjects provide spot-on examples and opportunities for preparing students for a rapidly changing technology landscape.

The U.S. Department of Education is committed to advancing STEM learning, offering federal resources "to assist educators in implementing effective approaches for improving STEM teaching and learning; facilitating the dissemination and adoption of effective STEM instructional practices nationwide; and promoting STEM education experiences that prioritize hands-on learning to increase student engagement and achievement" (U.S. Department of Education, n.d.).

Other agencies and companies are also collaborating to advance STEM. Read about what Macmillan Learning and Scientific American are doing around STEM and AI at the 2017 STEM Summit.

MACMILLAN AND SCIENTIFIC AMERICAN STEM SUMMIT 5.0 · · · · ·

Since artificial intelligence has a natural home in the word of education and academia, it is not surprising to see that many education companies are embracing and exploring this technology.

In fact, AI was a highlight of Macmillan Learning and Scientific American's 2017 STEM Summit. Co-founded by Susan Winslow, general manager of Macmillan Learning, and Mariette DiChristina, editor-in-chief of *Scientific American*, this annual summit brings together policymakers, thought leaders, and business partners within the education and research communities. As presenters and lecturers discuss how current technology trends will impact and transform the future of STEM education, artificial intelligence has become a hotly requested topic over the last few years.

Winslow explains:

> *We've found that the STEM Summit is an ideal environment for instructors and policymakers to discuss the risks, challenges, and possibilities artificial intelligence can pose to the learning experience. Instructors have shared their fears about being replaced by AI and we've also discussed some of the amazing things that are happening in classrooms today—like chatbots helping instructors answer the basic and repetitive questions for students, so that they can use office hours to tackle the more complex problems. We've also discussed the importance of human interaction in a digitized learning path. We explored the very real challenges of data mapping all the nuances that happen in learning (beyond just simple assessments) and why it's challenging for AI to show real learning gains (at this time).*

Among the 2017 STEM Summit presenters focused on AI were Ashok Goel, professor of computer science at the Georgia Institute of Technology and editor-in-chief of the Association for the Advancement of Artificial Intelligence journal *AI Magazine*; Carson Kahn, founder and CTO of Volley.com, a Silicon Valley artificial intelligence business with $5.3 million in disclosed seed financing from Zuckerberg Ventures, AI EdTech investors TAL Group (NYSE: XRS), and Reach Capital; and executives from Apple, Facebook, and Goldman Sachs.

During his 2017 STEM Summit presentation, "Jill and Friends: Virtual Tutors for Online Education" (**youtu.be/K-9qLZ2qdAk**), Goel shared his experience of creating an AI teaching assistant, Jill, for his popular online course on artificial intelligence (Leopold, 2016, **tinyurl.com/y9wlacu9**; Gose, 2016, **tinyurl.com/z2zpqek**). He created the assistant using Bluemix, an IBM platform that employs Watson and other IBM software to develop apps. More than 40,000 questions and answers from four semesters' worth of data were input, and the resulting program was tested and trained in a question-and-answer forum identical to the one used by students. When her answers were 97% accurate, Goel deemed Jill ready to use with his spring 2016 AI course (Leopold, 2016).

Goel did not initially tell the students in his AI course that their teaching assistant was actually AI at work. This experience presented him with unanticipated ethical questions that were important to explore and consider.

Watch Ashok Goel's TEDx talk about Jill and how AI can be used to scale personalized learning: **youtu.be/WbCguICyfTA**.

. . . .

STEM and Storytelling with Seeds

When people see the acronym "STEM" without knowing what it means, it evokes images of the stem of a plant. Seeds and plants, which represent growth and new life, have appeared in illustrations and word pictures across time. The case study below will include some examples of proverbs from around the world to illustrate the timelessness and global relevance of these teachings. The proverbs, sayings, stories, and teachings alone could turn into an entire project-based learning experience that delves into linguistics, world languages, geography, and social studies as well as STEM. You can ask your students how learning can be like starting with a seed that is planted. As you talk about the word "seed" and how it is represented in different languages (Figure 3.7), you can discuss natural language processing and how a computer might identify the word and the meaning and translate it to relate it back to AI. Students could embark on an investigation of communication and how spreading ideas to advance society can start small, with them. Once they know how to communicate their ideas effectively, they are planting seeds that can grow. They could discuss the analogy of a seed in relation to the movie *WALL-E*, exploring what the plant in the film represents and how sayings like "reaping what we sow" might connect to the film's deeper themes.

Figure 3.7
The word "seed" in
different languages.

llavor · sjeme · semínko · zaad · la graine

semente · σπόρος · Fræ · síolta · seme

frø · sămânţă семя · utsäde · semilla

זרע| · 種子 · シード · GiĐng · עֶרֶז · نائد

tohum · saad · abuur · mbegu · nkpuru

magbigay ng binhi · benih · benih

Susie Sung recently completed her second year of teaching six-year-olds using STEM, project-based learning, and design thinking. The previous year, she taught ages 9 and 10. She commented on the steep learning curve she experienced while transitioning between grade levels and said it felt overwhelming at times. There were moments when she didn't think she was successful or able to transition from the style she was used to teaching with to a very different way of guiding learning. She almost considered not teaching a second year with that style of learning. However, while some educators only want to teach one subject domain or one age level because there is a sense of security in always knowing what comes next, Susie was willing to be flexible. She presented on this topic with a panel of educators at Northwest Council for Computer Educators in February 2018 (**tinyurl.com/yc9kbcyq**), showing that educators new to this kind of learning can excel even if they do not feel confident at first. Knowing her challenges, setbacks, and vulnerability as an educator can provide valuable insight for those who are trying for the first time.

Susie shares the process she used for teaching the water cycle to her first-grade students. They also collaborated with a kindergarten class using Paint 3D (**education.microsoft.com/courses-and-resources/resources/3**).

CASE STUDY: WATER CYCLE UNIT ·····························

Susie Sung of Renton Prep in Renton, Washington

"A flower you plant may not necessarily bloom; but the seed of a tree you happen to drop may grow into a forest." —Chinese Proverb

We started by looking at how molecules are different in the different states of matter. Students organized beans to represent molecules in different states: solid, liquid, and gas. This gave them the ability to move objects with their hands and talk about it with each other in a collaborative space, an example of sociocultural learning (Vygotsky, 1989).

Figure 3.8
Students in kindergarten and first grade use beans to represent molecules.

We had fun observing the unique properties of water by estimating how many drops fit onto coins. I connected the lesson to our mathematics unit on money and understanding value, as well as the concept of estimation.

Students created the water cycle on Paint 3D, and then we also modeled the water cycle with paper materials and glued the parts onto a paper plate. Modeling first with a touch screen device on Paint 3D helped guide them to do it on paper. The technology allows them to visualize and problem-solve as they design their water cycle without fear of "messing up" on paper and having to erase and start all over again. It is also instantly gratifying to see it look like a water cycle right away with a few clicks.

Figure 3.9
The water cycle modeled on a paper plate.

We placed wet paper towels and seeds in closable plastic bags to observe what happened when they were in the window and received sunlight. We discussed what plants need to grow, and observed, and then drew our findings in Fresh Paint (**tinyurl.com/y9ea7g6t**). This is part of the observation process, recording variables, and documenting findings.

Our final project was to have the kids create a control experiment choosing one of the things that plants need to grow and testing it. For example, plants need water, so some students chose to put water in one cup of seeds and soda in another cup of seeds. Plants need soil, so some students chose to put sand in one cup of seeds and soil in another cup of seeds. They learned about variables and what it means to hold variables constant when using the scientific method. They recorded their findings using Fresh Paint on touch screen devices.

Then students used technology to create a presentation in Sway. Sway allows students to focus on the content while the program designs the layout for them. It is easy for them to drag and drop content that the program recommends based on the words and topics they type. There is a machine-learning algorithm in Sway that makes creating a presentation simple enough for my class to do independently. They can focus on communicating their ideas with machine learning assisting them, and I can focus my time on conversations and support instead of helping them design a polished project. Sway searches for images, video and descriptions from Creative Commons, meaning they are not restricted from use by copyright. Students are free to create and demonstrate their findings.

Malia was able to save her digital ink Fresh Paint observation drawing and drop the image into a media card so her work was captured within her final presentation. When Malia presses play, she has a digital artifact that is sharable on mobile devices. View Malia's Sway at **sway.com/H4AAI6j8ZmQ0Scrl?ref=Link**.

. . . .

"There will come a time when the seed will sprout." —Russian Proverb

Had Susie given up on a way of teaching that was new to her—had she not taken the challenge to teach first grade and risen to the challenge by adapting her fourth-grade content for six-year-olds—these children would have missed out on the richness of learning documented here. Not only did their seeds sprout, but so did their learning.

"Our examples are like seeds on a windy day, they spread far and wide."
—Nigerian Proverb

Because she made the effort to document her work and progress, Susie was able to capture her learning to illustrate the story of her growth as an educator. At the same time, she modeled the process of documenting learning for her students by taking photos, recording video, and collecting artifacts. She taught them how to capture their learning through photos, sketches, and writing with pencils so they could visually illustrate the learning process as they told the story of their exploration of water molecules, plants, and the scientific method. The children in Susie's class today are the children who will graduate in 2030.

HOW STEM WAS SEEN IN THIS UNIT

Learning crossed domains in a multi-modal way with hands, speech, and discussions, writing, modeling with physical representations as well as with Paint 3D, watching life grow with real seeds, and then experimenting using the scientific method. Watch another student video here: **youtu.be/geF0D7VI9SM**.

Below are some of the ways STEM played out in this unit:

Science: water molecules, water cycle, plant biology, scientific methods

Technology: research, FreshPaint, Paint 3D, digital photography, Sway

Engineering: problem-solving, design thinking, observation, modeling

Mathematics: estimation and money, geometry in Paint 3D creating water molecules

ISTE STANDARDS FOR STUDENTS DEMONSTRATED

The students in this lesson exemplified the ISTE Standards for Students in the following ways:

- They became empowered learners as they leveraged technology to take an active role in choosing, achieving and demonstrating competency in their learning goals, informed by the learning sciences.

- They became digital citizens by recognizing the responsibilities and opportunities of living, learning and working in an interconnected digital world, and they acted and modeled in ways that are safe, legal and ethical. They used the support of Sway to ensure their content was Creative Commons licensed.

- They were knowledge constructors by critically curating a variety of resources using digital tools, producing creative artifacts, and making meaningful learning experiences for themselves and others, as their learning has become a model for other educators at professional conferences.

- They became innovative designers by using a variety of technologies within a design process to identify and solve problems by creating new, useful, or imaginative solutions as six-year-olds.

- They practiced computational thinking by employing strategies for understanding and solving problems in ways that leverage the power of technological methods to develop and test solutions.

- They practiced creatively communicating using platforms, tools, styles, formats, and digital media appropriate to their goals, from FreshPaint and Paint 3D to Sway.

- They had an early introduction to becoming global collaborators by using digital tools to broaden their perspectives and enrich their learning by collaborating with others and working effectively in teams locally. Little did they know that their work would extend globally to impact educators from around the world. In that way, they can teach us, as adults, what they are capable of with STEM and project-based learning.

NEXT GENERATION SCIENCE STANDARDS ADDRESSED

Sometimes educators, parents, or administrators are concerned that STEM or project-based learning is not covering the same content as a textbook. That depends on how you design it and whether you keep the end goals in mind. The Next Generation Science Standards (NGSS) are designed to help keep learning goals at the forefront. They assist in seeing a bigger picture and combining more than one science domain, as well as recognizing other skills like language arts and communication. Look at the standard, 1-LS1-1 From Molecules to Organisms: Structures and Processes as it relates to Susie's water cycle unit: **tinyurl.com/y8u5az3h**. It includes science and engineering practices, disciplinary core ideas, and crosscutting concepts.

PROJECT-BASED LEARNING

New forms of education are emerging because of technology. Adaptive software is allowing students to advance more quickly in online courses and math. Dual enrollment programs are allowing students to overlap high school and college for a non-traditional educational trajectory. If AI can give us content quickly and more accurately than a human, how might education change?

Take 16-year-old Mia Britt, for example. She was in my middle school and high school cohort for four years in a multi-age setting. One of my goals for her cohort was to prepare them for early entry into a local community college, where they are dual-enrolled in high school and college. Their college tuition is paid for by the State of Washington after passing the entrance exam. By their senior year in high school, they will have the first two years of college completed with an associate in arts and sciences degree as well as a high school diploma. This allows them to transfer to a university with junior (third-year) status at age 18. I designed their cohort for 12- to 16-year-olds to be more similar to a graduate school course at the university level, in which they take responsibility for their learning, determine questions, align their content to standards, and co-design their project-based learning experience as well as the assessment criteria and rubrics. Creating non-traditional assessments and accurately assessing their own work requires students to become knowledge constructors, empowered learners, innovative designers, computational thinkers, global collaborators, digital citizens, and creative communicators.

To demonstrate their knowledge, students had multiple opportunities to speak with industry professionals and provide feedback on newly developing technology, lead their portfolio reviews with their parents to explain their learning process, and speak to educators at professional conferences across the U.S. Since student voice is important to a discussion on what we want our young people to be able to do when they complete formal education, I invited Mia to describe the project-based learning approach to educators who may not be familiar with it, or for educators who would like to see a student perspective on PBL.

STUDENT VOICE: MIA BRITT ·

Project-based learning is an approach to education in which a project is assigned (to an individual or team) to demonstrate learning through concepts such as graphic design, various types of media, short videos, skits, etc.

Project-based learning isn't a substitute for traditional tests you study for, but it adds another dimension and way of learning for students. Through different projects, important information can be learned from students being creative, instead of a student studying a load of information for a test the night before and not remembering anything afterward.

Since projects are different from traditional tests and have more components, students have to think through more concepts. This supports our ability to be computational thinkers and to think critically. We don't have someone to tell us the answers every step of the way, so we need to learn skills to identify the problem and make the plans to solve that problem. We learn to identify the topics we need to research in order to get the information we need, use technology to find helpful sources, then apply our learning to solve the problem. Creativity is part of project-based learning. We need to reach the goal, but we can choose how we get there.

Although project-based learning has a lot of positives, there are a few downsides:

- Creating *too* many projects could become stressful.

- If students don't have practice or aren't familiar with PBL, they can become stressed and want to give up, especially people who are used to memorizing easily to get good grades and see that as successful learning.

- There should be a balance between projects and tests so that students don't forget how to take them.

- Teachers should help regulate team members. Without proper enforcement, some team members can let others do all the work and not learn for themselves.

- Flexibility is important, but don't allow too much flexibility for students. Give some constraints.

- Technical difficulties can be frustrating, but since technology isn't perfected and it is still being developed, they are bound to happen.

CREATIVE CONSTRAINTS

As Mia said, too much flexibility isn't always helpful. In real life, projects can be restricted by a multitude of factors. There are requirements and limitations we have to address to accomplish a goal. Students need to practice this early and often, realizing that constraints are drivers of discovery and invention. Watch the TED-Ed video on Creative Constraints: **tinyurl.com/y827k46c**.

WHERE DO I START?

Here are some resources to get you started with project-based learning. You can read more about project-based learning at **cultofpedagogy.com/project-based-learning**.

- Pick a topic. For example:
  - Paper Tree Project: **youtu.be/ypd8lDhPxQo**
  - Early Childhood STEM: The Three Billy Goats Gruff: Children's Literature and STEM: **youtu.be/_i5pZLj84yl**
  - Life Cycle of a Plant: STEAM and digital animation: **youtu.be/geF0D7Vl9SM**
  - SpinoDino: Rap, Music, Paleontology, History, Language Arts, and Video Production: **youtu.be/B-ro1TOElrQ**
  - The Little Book Project – The Little Prince: Storytelling and Digital Literacy: **sway.office.com/dTo7zMhK6w1Br2Cb**
  - Indigenous People Double Exposure: Math, Art, Culture and Technology: **sway.office.com/CCTzmRrQ9LPyBROA**
  - Logic and Argumentation: **sway.office.com/PbVMBRHCSyFa8e7r**
  - Graphite Grid Picture: Science, Technology, Engineering, Art, Math: **sway.office.com/0sO7CNLVWlhhGPlJ**
  - Pompeii and Seattle: History, Social Studies, Geography, Arts, Science: **sway.office.com/hJeH7sAFxpsTBRzB**
  - Besiege and Physics: Physics, Gaming, and Mentoring: **sway.office.com/jqJyNiScemHNOY64**
  - Explaining STEM to Adults—A collaborative project: **sway.office.com/Oi1OeB0MvLxakiyv**
- Have an open discussion about the topic (raising hands, writing down questions to share with the group).
- Have the students pick an overarching theme to focus their project on. For example, in the Paper Tree Project above, the overarching theme was how nature can influence architectural engineering choices when building structures such as the Sagrada Familia in Barcelona, Spain. It can also influence computer animation, such as when Pixar uses the approximation of a parabola to help model realistic blades of grass. In the Children's Literature and STEM project, the theme was recreating the

bridge from the Three Billy Goats Gruff. In the SpinoDino rap, a National Geographic Live student matinee on Spinosaurus discoveries became the theme, and each student chose how they combined more than one subject to demonstrate learning. In the Pompeii project, the theme was volcanoes and comparing and contrasting the port cities of Pompeii, Italy, and Seattle, Washington.

- Give the students a guide; teach them how to create their own rubric so there are no surprises when the project is due and assessed. Students can vote on the final criteria and hold each other accountable. They can't blame the teacher since they helped create it.

- Introduce them to new tools, such as Sway (**sway.com**) and Microsoft Translator (**translator.microsoft.com**) and let them learn the tools along the way as part of their project-based learning.

We have learned that machines are capable of immense processing at deeper and quicker levels than humans in specific domains. However, at this point, machines aren't good at transferring knowledge from one domain to another. This is where you can help your learners amplify the skills that they can perform better than a machine. There are many exceptional design thinking, project-based learning, and STEM resources online. Combining these ways of thinking with ethical considerations is crucial to developing well-rounded students who are prepared for a world with increasing AI—now and in the future.

Nullius in Verba: Take Nobody's Word for It

Earlier, we noted that it is challenging to determine a path or approach to teaching a developing content area. We teach theoretical science concepts as fact, have students memorize them, and test them on their memory. In my anthropology and pre-medical courses at the University of Washington, I asked how to study for certain theories since multiple sources provided different answers and both of those answers showed up on multiple choice tests. It wasn't until university that I realized the reason some things changed was because they were theories—albeit ones that had strong support—and not facts. Yet prior to that question, no educator had explained that what I was memorizing was the best information we had at that point, or that things could change as more knowledge developed.

Recently, there have been new findings in neuroscience that contradicted what I spent hours memorizing in university—things that I understood were facts. As an educator, I made the decision to help my students begin to question what may seem to be fact. Even the slight shift to understanding the difference between a fact and a theory that is supported by evidence can help students think more deeply and learn to question. From history, I wanted students to understand multiple perspectives and realized that who tells the story has an influence on how something is identified as a fact. In science, what we know is based on evidence that supports the claim. I wanted students to explore controversial topics and hear how other people questioned and challenged ideas, and then I asked them to evaluate those claims. If they made a claim or chose a claim to believe, I wanted them to support their claim with evidence. If they read something online, I wanted them to question not only the fact, but also the source, potential bias, and even the information provided by people they see as authorities.

So much of education trains students to take in information and not question, to memorize and trust authority for facts, because the authority has been trained and has more knowledge than the student. However, as we can see, machines are quickly overtaking a human's ability to sort through large amounts of data. This means that with the assistance of a machine's search features, an inexperienced person may find new information that an authority may not yet know about. That doesn't mean our job as educators is obsolete. It means we need to shift our approach to teaching, and not just for the sake of teaching for a future that includes intelligent machines. We need to teach our young people to question.

AN EXERCISE IN QUESTIONING SOURCES

It is easy to tell your students to question sources. It can feel like a successfully completed instructional lesson on evaluating sources and not believing everything you read—until you try a different kind of "test." This activity can be illuminating and helpful for starting discussions. Being able to question is an important part of evaluating media and gaining knowledge.

PROCEDURE

1. Provide students with the following link: **zapatopi.net/treeoctopus**.
2. Tell students their task is to come back with three things they learned from the article and then the class will discuss.

3. You can create an online form for students to fill in or ask them to write their responses on a piece of paper.

4. Tell students they have the option of using only the source you provided, or they can research on their own.

Spoiler Alert for Educators: You are directing students to a hoax website for the Pacific Northwest Tree Octopus. A quick search returns results identifying it as a hoax.

DISCUSSION QUESTIONS FOR STUDENTS:

- How many of you chose to focus on the link I provided? Why?
- What most surprised you about what you read?
- What did you learn from this experience?
- What would you do differently next time?
- How many of you chose to do your own research in addition to the link I provided? Why?

IMPLEMENTATION TIPS:

Intentionally leave the task vague: Identify three things you learned. Why? You want to give students the chance to practice questioning information and sources.

As an educator creating this assessment for ages 10 through 13, I was fully expecting my students to come back with laughter and tell me how ridiculous the website was. After all, we live in the Pacific Northwest, and although over 90% of my students had parents who were not born in the U.S., at least half of them were born in the region, where there are many pine trees. I didn't know whether to laugh or cry when I read the three things they learned: "I learned that octopus can actually live in pine trees. I didn't know that before." "I didn't know there was an organization to help save the endangered tree octopus. We should join the cause and raise money to help the endangered animals." "I didn't know about the mating habits of these octopus. I always used to think they lived in water and not in trees, but I've learned something new today."

Not one student wrote the answers I was hoping—no, expecting—to see. The answers I wanted should have included (in no particular order) any of the following: 1) I learned that hoax websites can look professional. 2) I learned it is important to do my own research. 3) I learned that if someone gives me a link, it does not mean the information is accurate. 4) I learned that when a teacher asks me what I learned, it does not necessarily mean to report facts; there are other things I can learn. 5) I learned that it is important to ask myself and other people questions about what I read. 6) I have learned that even if I know from experience, it is easy to be fooled by media.

This challenge was created to help students practice investigating in a place of ambiguity, and to question, research, and understand what counts as learning.

. . . .

In a personal conversation with Hidekazu Shoto, he described a phrase they use at their school:

心のコップを上にしよう

"An upside-down cup cannot be filled" is a traditional idea that educators value at Ritsumeikan Primary School. If a student turns their metaphorical cup right side up, it allows them to accept knowledge, understanding, and even love or respect. This idea applies to all aspects of life and relationships, both local and global, as they teach children to become globally minded citizens. Their mission clearly states what they want their young people to be able to do when they complete their formal education. Their goal is not to have young people give robots the hard work; rather, students learn how to take care of their environment.

They learn about their culture and history, their values and ethics, and yet they have also embraced project-based learning and STEM through gaming in the classroom as they learn about UNESCO World Heritage sites and share their first-person perspective with others around the world. Students build and communicate with each other, learning about each other's lives.

Beginning this chapter on approaches to teaching AI with the story of a school that teaches the Way of Tea conveyed a message about the value of "restoring old as old" while looking forward to what the future holds and preparing students to look beyond their own geographical borders. Ritsumeikan Primary's approach to learning, whether they intentionally planned it or not, is preparing students to approach AI with an emphasis on humanity. Connecting multiple domains, merging ideas and concepts—AI can't transfer learning the way humans can. In this increasingly complex world, Ritsumeikan Primary maintains a balance, returning to harmony (和 wa), respect (敬 kei), purity (清 sei), and tranquility (寂 jaku). The tea ceremony is an event that honors relationship, supported by a philosophy that each gathering should be valued because that moment in time is unique and can never be replicated.

As an educator, you have the opportunity to develop an approach to teaching AI in which you value each moment with your students, knowing that it is unique. That moment can bring its own failures, successes, small victories, and unexpected moments of profound learning. This is where you have the capacity to exceed the ability of a machine.

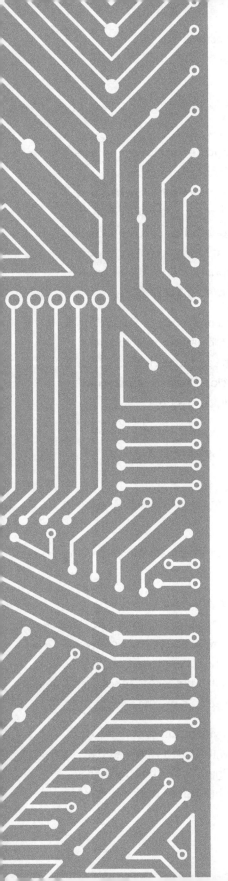

CHAPTER 4
How AI Can Support Student Learning

Expanding Horizons with Storytelling and AI

DRAMATIS PERSONAE

CAMILLE MERCADO: A 13-year-old student

MICHELLE ZIMMERMAN: Author and educator

SCENE

Camille, a middle school student, is co-presenting with her teacher, Michelle Zimmerman, at the ISTE 2012 conference at the San Diego Convention Center in California.

TIME: June, 2012

ACT II

Scene 4

SETTING: ISTE's annual conference and exposition is the world's most comprehensive education technology event. Around 18,000 educators, tech coordinators, teacher educators, administrators, and industry and government representatives have gathered from all over the world. Leslie Conery, ISTE deputy CEO and conference chair, has announced that the conference's theme, "Expanding Horizons," aims to "create a conference experience that focuses on how educators can fuel students' passion to learn. We believe that a comprehensive, digital-age education expands students' horizons and better prepares them to succeed in college, career, and civic life" (ISTE, 2012).

AT RISE: Camille and her teacher are putting the final touches on a poster session Camille has coauthored. Aligned to the ISTE Standards for Students, the presentation focuses on her year-long mentorship with Tracy, a three-year-old English Language Learner whose family is from Vietnam. Camille rarely volunteers to speak in class, but this opportunity to share her experience with adult educators is too important to pass up.

Warm sea breezes rustle the palm trees as a glint of sun breaks through the leaves and splinters the light and shadows cast on the sidewalk outside the San Diego Convention Center.

It is Camille's first conference. Located in a different state, it required her to take a plane from Seattle, Washington, to San Diego, California.

It is also her first time presenting outside of the classroom—and her first time presenting to adults other than her teacher. This is a big deal.

Before presenting, she took the lead on writing the conference proposal, which was accepted in an adult category. With scaffolding from her teacher, Camille wrote what she thought was important for teachers to know and described how she used technology to capture her mentoring interactions with Tracy throughout the school year. Camille's parents did not think she would speak to adults, even up until the moment they saw her engage in conversation with educators at ISTE. They are amazed. So are the educators.

When Camille talks to educators, she does not just talk about video editing or mentoring Tracy. She talks about what she did as a mentor and how it aligned with the ISTE Standards for Students. She talks about becoming a better digital citizen through her experiences. She talks about the skills she learned that made her better at critical thinking, collaboration, creativity, and communication. She talks about using digital ink and a relational connection to elicit words from a girl who was reluctant to speak English out loud.

It started with a squiggle on a screen. Camille drew the squiggle to show Tracy how the touch screen and pen on her device worked. The learning continued as Camille modeled and discussed the tool, then asked Tracy to draw something with it. When Tracy got stuck, Camille supported her, helping her complete the drawing by adding an eye for the turtle, then a red turtle shell. She deleted the image and gave Tracy the chance to draw something entirely on her own. At the end of a successful drawing, Camille holds up her hand for a high five. Tracy looks at Camille's hand, smiles, acknowledging the gesture as a sign of congratulations and a job well done, then completes the motion of a high five with a huge smile on her face.

Because Camille's computer had a camera, she was able to record their interactions. The footage shows evidence to support claims of Tracy's progress from the first recording, when Camille asked her to draw something and inquired about her favorite colors, to the comparison video she recorded at the end of the school year, in which she interviewed Tracy. Finally, Camille shows the video in which she engaged in early literacy by co-constructing a story with Tracy taking the lead, speaking sentences in English, laughing, and smiling. Camille only needed to step in to provide minor support.

End Scene 4

Foundations for Human-Computer Interaction and STEM Learning

The story in Scene 4 was part of an original research study I conducted, published in Springer's *Human-Computer Interaction Series* (Zimmerman, 2016). As discussed in the last chapter, preparing students for a future in which humans interact with intelligent machines needs to start with—and emphasize and amplify—aspects of our humanity that we have the unique capability to develop. Machines are exceptional at certain tasks, and they are getting better. However, if our brains have the capacity to develop empathy and relationships, transfer learning across multiple settings, remain flexible as we adapt to unexpected responses, and use storytelling to help support learning and remembering, we should support that learning. Where Camille did not appear to excel in traditional test-taking, she far exceeded expectations in her ability to leverage technology to support human growth, development, and relationship. Fostering STEM skills often begins with some form of relationship.

Technology helped Camille facilitate both human interaction and English dialogue. She began from a relational standpoint, by getting to know what Tracy liked and disliked. She accurately assessed Tracy's skill level and provided support (Vygotsky, 1987). She got to know how Tracy thought (Fair, Vandermaas-Peeler, Beaudry & Dew, 2005). From there, Camille encouraged Tracy when she hesitated and provided further scaffolding. When she met resistance, Camille either increased support or transitioned to a new activity. Technology provided a basic blank canvas for Camille and Tracy to draw on as they shared knowledge and co-created meaning.

Tracy's preschool teacher also taught Camille in kindergarten. A proficient reader back then, Camille later demonstrated a strong command of phonemic awareness as she guided Tracy. Whether Camille realized it or not, many of the methods she used in supporting Tracy were identical to the methods she experienced as a kindergarten student.

Enright (2011) talked about language for everyday interactions, called **basic interpersonal conversation skills (BICS)**. Developmentally, BICS come before **cognitive academic language proficiency (CALP)**. Learners need a foundation of "well-developed interpersonal languages (BICS) with the help of formal instruction" before CALP can become solid. Camille was helping Tracy develop BICS and CALP simultaneously through conversation and literacy strategies. This type of human interaction and support provides a foundation for fostering STEM learning.

Learning as a Sociocultural Process

Many people in STEM fields have been inspired by someone they admire or who personally invested in them. Recall Nile Wilson's story from Chapter 1, and the encouragement she received as she explored her interest in STEM. She mentioned her love of working with people as they come together to solve complex problems that cannot be addressed through a narrow focus. This is very human.

While machines can excel in areas of narrow focus, humans can bring pieces of disparate information together to construct new knowledge and innovate. We can find connections across seemingly very different things, like tea and a discussion on AI. We have the ability to become creative in the ways we communicate, respond to unexpected or novel situations, and construct new knowledge. Tracy's learning began with a digital ink squiggle on a screen and ended with an imaginative story in which she invented the spelling of the name of her princess—and this as a bilingual student mastering both Vietnamese and English. As her mentor, Camille was successful in capturing the child's progress in a way that had not been done in a class full of students. Without the footage Camille recorded, Tracy's teacher would not have known how much skill Tracy had, and I would not have known how much skill Camille had.

Camille will finish her associate degree in computer science and transfer to the University of Washington in Seattle to pursue a bachelor's degree in informatics, an applied form of information science that involves interaction between humans and information through interfaces and technology systems. Here is what she had to say about sharing her experience with Tracy at the ISTE conference:

> Being able to present this research with Michelle Zimmerman at the ISTE conference in 2012 was an impactful experience for me. At the time, I never really understood the importance of how my class would spend a year being mentors to preschoolers. I just thought of it as a way that preschoolers can have the ability to become friendlier with older kids or adults; but it became way more than that. Devoting my time that summer to review the information I gathered with my preschooler, Tracy, made me understand the importance of technology alongside its ability to improve social interactions and learning with children. There was a significant improvement with Tracy and especially myself after partaking in this research. What we've gathered was not exposed to a lot of educators, so the ability to present this in a panel seemed like we made a breakthrough in technology involvement with students as well as the integration of using STEM outside of learning.

> With what I've learned and experienced with this research, it was easier to apply STEM in high school, which helped me excel in the technology academy I was in and gave me the confidence to practice my public speaking by becoming the school's video production lead anchor. These opportunities led me to become a show announcer for a city-wide tech showcase, an event giving students and educators alike an opportunity to present their own research like I did.

> As I would introduce different students' projects at the showcase, I could not help but reflect on my middle school self and how far I've come since then. Knowing that these kids showcasing what they've learned are in the same mindset as I was in ISTE. They do not know that the knowledge they're presenting can also leave a breakthrough in the ever-continuous research of technology in classrooms. (Camille Mercado, personal communication, 2018)

As we consider a future that involves human and machines interacting on increasingly complex levels, we need to consider more than just the intersection of cognitive systems, robotics, and machine learning. We need to consider human learning as a social and cultural process. Preparing our young people for this kind of future should include opportunities for them to learn about learning, explore how to learn with others, and discover how to guide the learning of others. Unless people decide to enter a teaching or training profession, rarely do they have the opportunity to experience what it is like to shift from the role of a learner to the role of teaching someone else in a formal learning environment. Most often, students have the experience of being the one trained—the learner who memorizes, understands, and repeats. If machines can also be trained, learn, memorize, and repeat, then students need to expand their capacity beyond a machine's by learning to teach as well as to learn.

Lacina (2004) points out that isolated drill and practice is not an effective way to improve academic achievement. While students still need basic skills before they can create and innovate, repetition and repeated practice throughout the year should not be isolated from human interaction, nor should the skills rehearsed be isolated from a context in which students apply those skills.

In an article called *The 7 Most Important STEM Skills We Should Be Teaching Our Kids* (Adams, 2017), the author lists skills such as problem-solving, creativity, argumentation, intellectual curiosity, and flexibility. Two other skills listed by Adams in his 2017 article are statistics and data-driven decision making. Teaching these skills not only helps students understand their relationship with AI, but it prepares them to excel in a world in which AI is ubiquitous and constantly advancing.

There are many pathways and approaches to learning about AI. Among them are storytelling, personalized learning, differentiated instruction, and robotics.

Storytelling and Preparing For AI

For some, storytelling and computer science are very different skill sets that do not seem to go together. Many children have been coached to choose one or the other, not both. But read Jonathan Grudin's story. Ever since he could read, Jonathan loved to write fiction and non-fiction.

"I like resolving mysteries, solving problems that present themselves, and finding patterns," Jonathan said. When he discovered computer programming as a teen-ager, "storybook magic became real: I could have a thought and see it come to life, with consequences that sometimes were anticipated, and sometimes not" (Grudin, 2018).

As educators, we know how powerful storytelling can be in the learning process. Storytelling can help us remember. It can become part of our culture (Nasir, Rosebery, Warren, & Lee, 2006) and tradition, as various cultures express wisdom through oral and written stories (Choi, 2015; Faggella, 2015; Tillman, 2006). To tell stories is human. If we could develop a machine or system that could imitate a storytelling human, would it equate to an intelligent entity that could pass on wisdom the way a human can (Faggella, 2015)?

When we talk about **natural intelligence**, we are referring to what humans and animals are naturally capable of. AI refers to a machine's attempt at replicating or augmenting that natural intelligence. This is something the AI community wrestles with. Some in the field focus solely on reproducing human intelligence. However, most of the work today is aimed at getting computers to do things people cannot do, or finding ways to do things differently; these experts are not expecting to replicate human intelligence (J. Grudin, personal communication, May 5, 2018).

Grudin has helped a new generation of young people discover a passion for human-computer interaction. His love of storytelling and coding as a child gave him a solid foundation for the work he is doing as principal researcher at Microsoft, with a focus on education. My students and I had the opportunity to interact with him in person at the ninth Workshop on the Impact of Pen and Touch Technology on Education in 2015. One of the first things that impressed me about Jonathan was his ability to maintain a balance between theory and practice as he related to my students on a very human level and guided them through design thinking and STEM challenges (Zimmerman, 2016; Gonzalvo, et. al., 2016; Valentine, Conrad, Oduola, & Hammond, 2016).

Grudin has worked with AI groups since the late 1970s. Many educational processes, methods, and paradigms cycle through the decades (Grudin, 2017), as do advancements in AI. The technology flourishes for a time, then seems to flag as we enter another AI winter (J. Grudin, personal communication, May 5, 2017). When people become excited about AI's potential, AI experiences a wave of enthusiasm. The complexity becomes vivid, and enthusiasm wanes as a new AI winter arrives and funding becomes harder to find. Then advancements in technology bring new promises of exponential growth (Kurzweil, 2001), and the cycle of the AI seasons continues. Roger Shank (2018) cautions that overpromising the current capabilities of AI can usher in another AI winter; he advocates for accurately identifying AI's current capabilities and maintaining transparency regarding its limitations. Preparing young people for a future with AI should include a long-term vision so they do not give up during cycles of decreased funding or apparent slowing of progress.

Although some may see the cycle of AI summers and winters as discouraging, there is a beauty in it as we gain a deeper and more profound appreciation for the complexity of the human mind and how it works (Allen, 2011), as well as the nuances of sociocultural interaction (A. Goel, personal communication, May, 2018). That knowledge can inspire us as educators to discover new ways to maximize the potential of the human brain (Campbell, 2017) and challenge us to amplify the aspects that make us uniquely human, rather than teaching students the most basic processing tasks or asking them only to memorize and repeat content.

DESIGN THINKING, SYSTEMS THINKING, AND CITIZEN SCIENCE · · ·

Amplify students' uniquely human capabilities with resources for:

- Design thinking: **tinyurl.com/y75b8a5d**
- Systems thinking: **drawtoast.com**
- Citizen science: **tinyurl.com/y8th3hf2**

Personalized Learning

This chapter opened with a story about personalized learning that was not just personalized—it also became very personal. Although definitions of personalized learning may vary, one thing they have in common is that students engaging in this type of learning are not all doing the same thing at the same time. The learning reflects something about their culture, passion, unique situation, challenge, or direction for the future. It may be the way a student frames an assignment or goal, or it could be gradually releasing control as an educator to allow the student to practice more self-regulation, self-direction, and knowledge construction.

Unlike more traditional approaches to education, personalized learning focuses on the human element of learning—the unique needs and differences of students as they explore the depths of their own curiosity. As we work to develop the capabilities in today's young people that will distinguish them from ever-smarter machines, personalized learning offers a pathway for allowing vital skills like creativity and critical thinking to flourish. At the same time, AI is enabling greater levels of personalization than ever before, with tools that expand the teacher's capacity to allow students to explore different avenues of inquiry, while gleaning valuable insights about how each child learns.

There are a range of YouTube video producers who have reached a wide audience and added diversity to personalized learning pathways. I had the opportunity to meet Jabril at South by Southwest Edu in Austin, Texas in 2018. He spoke on AI and was a participant at the AI Summit where I presented. We struck up a conversation in the hallway on shifting approaches to preparing young people for AI. Jabril is a digital media producer who prides himself on visually exemplifying information and exploring new digital media frontiers. For the past 10 years, Jabril has been practicing the craft of storytelling through digital media, which has given him great leverage in pursuing his goal of teaching kids to love learning. Growing up, Jabril did not have many role models to show him that learning is an incredibly thrilling process, and so equipped with his media experience, a passion to give others what he did not have, and a personal YouTube channel, he strives show others that education can be a fun and rewarding process. He has produced videos to inspire young people to investigate machine learning and artificial intelligence.

UNDERSTANDING AI ·

Explore Jabril's STEM video on machine learning and AI, and find out how he got interested in neural networks. He also discusses how he improved his math skills to achieve his goal of making a machine-learning game:

- "Writing My First Machine Learning Game": **youtu.be/ZX2Hyu5WoFg**
- "Training My First Machine Learning Game": **youtu.be/OpodKCR6P-M**
- "Finishing My First Machine Learning Game": **youtu.be/GDy45vT1xIA**
- "Post Mortem for My First Machine Learning Game": **youtu.be/g-HePO2bcTY**

· ·

As an educator, exploring this new frontier of personalized learning can feel difficult to grasp. How do we maintain control over what everyone is doing if not everyone is on the same textbook page at the same time, working from one set of correct answers to a test that can be standardized?

Successful personalized learning includes the following characteristics:

- Content and standards are met through students pursuing their interests and expanding their abilities in authentic, real-world activities.

- Rather than conveying knowledge, educators support, coach, and facilitate students.

- Students build creativity, critical thinking, and self-efficacy as they define and regulate their own learning path to achieve goals that have been established.

- Technology affords students the ability to choose what, how, and why they demonstrate their learning.

- Learning occurs in cycles rather than a linear progression from receiving content to being tested on the content. Digital tools help students and teachers assess strengths and weaknesses throughout the learning cycle.

- Skills and subject areas to be learned are clearly identified and then measured through evidence of proficiency in skills and understanding.

- Students and teachers integrate technology throughout the experience to support learning, choosing the tools that best match the task.

- Personalized learning does not replace educators, but it does provide data and strategies to help educators know when to intervene and offer redirection or more support, and when to let students self-regulate, practice autonomy, and pace themselves as they make intentional decisions about their own progress and success in meeting goals.

When students become knowledge constructors and innovative designers, they take control of their learning and are able to demonstrate their progress. Look at these examples of how students used Sway to create a portfolio to demonstrate their personalized learning pathway:

Sharice Lee, Grade 8: **sway.com/49wJZa2zEHqiFu8W**

Afomeya Hailu, Grade 9: **sway.com/OoH8PFbrvgnW3dqF**

PERSONALIZED LEARNING THROUGH IMPACT · · · · · · · · · · · · · · · · · ·

Listen to students explain the ImpaCT program in South Africa for English and Math support: **youtu.be/z6BEdNsWkmI**. What elements of personalized learning can you detect as they speak?

· ·

AI can support personalized learning through programs like Mia Learning (**mialearning.com**) as well as virtual personal assistants. Pixar in a Box (**khanacademy.org/partner-content/pixar**) offers personalized learning pathways. Khan Academy (**khanacademy.org**) is another program that supports personalized learning.

Tools like Sway can quickly help students personalize the design and communication of their newly created knowledge, while keeping the format and delivery of the content consistent. Sway uses machine-learning algorithms to support search and design, among other features. In essence, the machine learning helps shoulder some of the workload, providing a professional, polished design so students can focus on creating personalized content.

ETHNOGRAPHY PROJECT BY AFOMEYA HAILU · · · · · · · · · · · · · · · · · ·

Explore an example of personalized learning by Afomeya Hailu: **sway.com/ D6ksyWgZeKYSI2IC**. This ethnography assignment was a personalized, project-based learning experience anchored in social studies. How many of the ISTE Standards for Students can you find in Afomeya's ethnography on her family's history and culture in Ethiopia?

· ·

Differentiated Instruction

If you have taught mathematics, you know that you will never have a classroom of students in which all arrive with the same prior knowledge, ask the same questions, work at the same pace, or approach practicing and studying for math in the same way. As an educator, if you are given freedom in how you choose to teach math, you may have several options to consider. One option could be to maintain consistency and cohesiveness by ensuring all students keep the same pace and progress through content together. Another option is to allow students to progress at their own pace. If you have ever tried this method, you know how difficult it can be—no, humanly impossible—to keep track of where everyone is at any given moment and assess sometimes drastically different content at the same time. Differentiated learning often involves bouncing between topics to answer questions and support student learning just in time for the next wave of questions.

Solutions now exist to support differentiated learning using the basic foundational components of AI. McGraw Hill Mathematics has an adaptive program called ALEKS. Fifteen-year-old Rhonwyn Fleming describes her first year using ALEKS to learn math:

> *ALEKS is an online program that teaches students math. At the beginning of the school year, the students each take a placement test, which chooses questions based upon which ones the student got correct. The program then places the student in a course; for high schoolers, it could be Algebra, Algebra II, Geometry, or higher math. Each course not only covers Common Core State Standards concepts, but also fills in any gaps there may be in the student's previous mathematical education. Since each course is tailored to the student's needs, and therefore individualized, each student can go at his or her own pace. This is very helpful because some students understand some concepts right away, but some may need more time to really think it through. Along with exercises, ALEKS gives a short explanation of the topic as well as other resources for further reading. Because of this, a math teacher does not have to give a lesson every day; instead they act as a facilitator. This is beneficial because students no longer need to listen to lessons that they could either be bored with or not understand.*
>
> *ALEKS also teaches valuable skills like time management and student-driven learning. ALEKS displays how many topics are left in the course, so it is easy to figure out how many must be done each week in order to finish the course by the end of the school year. ALEKS also utilizes a natural human desire to see things completed. By setting a goal, it motivates the student to work, so he or she can see the course through to the end. Without the motivation and time management skills, it would be very hard to complete the course. (Rhonwyn Fleming, Personal Communication, 2018)*

Afomeya Hailu has used ALEKS for a couple years. This is what she had to say about it:

> *I was introduced to ALEKS when I was in seventh grade. When we first began using it, I was very skeptical about how it worked and the accuracy of the program. I had only known math class as a place where the teacher taught a lesson, and you completed an assignment. I did not know a math class where you were able to move at your own pace and complete as many math courses as you want. That all changed when we began using ALEKS. ALEKS is an online math course that allows teachers to keep track of their students' progress in various math courses. You are able to complete your math course*

at your own speed. This means in one school year you can complete multiple courses, or just one. At our school, we are required to complete at least one math course each year, and 10 topics and 2.5 hours each week. These are the only requirement we have when it comes to ALEKS. In each ALEKS math course, there are multiple sections, such as Linear Equations or Real Numbers. Each of these sections has multiple topics. For each topic, you are given a lesson and two to three questions to answer. If you get a certain number of questions correct, you are able to pass the topic. If you get a question wrong, you are given one more chance to answer it, and if you get that wrong you are shown another explanation. After a certain amount of topics and hours spent in an ALEKS course, each student is given a mandatory Knowledge Check. During the Knowledge Check, you are tested on the topics you have learned recently. Once you finish the test you might have to revisit a few topics based on whether or not you got the answers correct. One thing I have found is that with ALEKS I often forget the topic I learned. When I have in-class lessons, similar lessons are taught throughout the week or section so the math is drilled into my brain. Many of the topics in ALEKS are only two to three questions, so I do not get as much practice.

Throughout the years, I have noticed that when ALEKS is used hand-in-hand with in-class lessons and projects, it helps me understand everything more clearly. The in-class lessons help me understand the base components I need for my grade-level math, and ALEKS helps me move faster or slower in my personal math courses. Times where I only have ALEKS are often spent completing topics but never remembering what I learned. When I only have in-class math lessons I find myself getting bored and restricted. When these are put together, I find it more effective for myself. (Afomeya Hailu, personal communication, 2018)

ALEKS

- Discover the science behind ALEKS: **aleks.com/about_aleks/Science_Behind_ALEKS.pdf**.
- See ALEKS in action: **youtu.be/EQ9PkS2aX7U**.
- Find out how ALEKS works: **youtu.be/-1Q4jRbpODQ**.
- Read the research ALEKS is based on: **aleks.com/k12/research_behind_aleks**.

For early childhood learning, Sesame Workshop has been exploring AI in connection with learning to read. It is supported by IBM Watson. IBM Watson and Sesame Workshop completed their initial pilot with Georgia's Gwinnett County Public Schools, one of the nation's top urban school districts, exploring how the industry's first cognitive vocabulary-learning app performed with young students. When humans interact with intelligent machines, both learn. The machines learn from the students, and the students learn from the machines. Read more here: **tinyurl.com/y9u7xtsk**.

SESAME WORKSHOP

Sesame Workshop uses an iterative research model—inform, improve, measure, repeat—to devise developmentally appropriate ways of supporting personalized learning for very young children. Their approach looks at how young children respond to content, then addresses common questions, clears up misconceptions, and scaffolds challenging concepts. They harness the emotional side of learning by attaching laughter and emotion to key learning components. Along the way, they build in support for cognitive academic language proficiency (CALP) and conversational language (BICS), modeled by the characters investigating and discussing their learning as young children watch. Their iterative model not only helps refine the learning approach, but it helps adults differentiate instruction as they move toward AI-assisted literacy skill development. Read more about how Sesame Workshop is intentional in their approach to learning: **sesameworkshop.org/what-we-do/our-research-model**.

ACCESSIBILITY AND DIFFERENTIATED INSTRUCTION

The Microsoft course "Accessibility Tools: Meeting the Needs of Diverse Learners" (**education.microsoft.com/gettrained/accessibility**) explores features that are already built into Office 365 tools, which use natural language processing and machine learning to support accessibility for people with dyslexia and vision impairment, as well as young students who need reading assistance. Microsoft's mission is to empower all people and organizations to achieve more; the classroom is no different. Microsoft Windows and Windows-based applications like Office, together with other assistive technologies, offer features that make computers easier to use for everyone—giving teachers the opportunity to provide personalized learning, and giving students an improved experience and equal opportunity in the classroom.

- See a range of accessibility technologies in action: **microsoft.com/en-us/accessibility**.

- Learn more about OneNote Immersive Reader: **tinyurl.com/ycl4qejr**.

- Watch a video about OneNote Immersive Reader: **youtu.be/ZrO-IlIKjbw**.

Robotics

Robots are not synonymous with AI, but AI is one component of intelligent machines that interact with the physical world. As we prepare students for a future that integrates robotics and cognitive systems like IBM Watson with machine learning, it is good to expose them to robotics. Learning-by-doing activities are part of the Building Machines that Emulate Humans lesson offered by Microsoft. This lesson shows you how to build a sensor to control a robotic hand (Figure 4.1). Aligned with Next Generation Science Standards, the lesson plan celebrates real-world scenarios in which engineers and scientists build tools that allow surgeons to perform remotely controlled surgeries or astronauts to control rovers in space. Learn more about the lesson at **tiny.cc/27xr0y**.

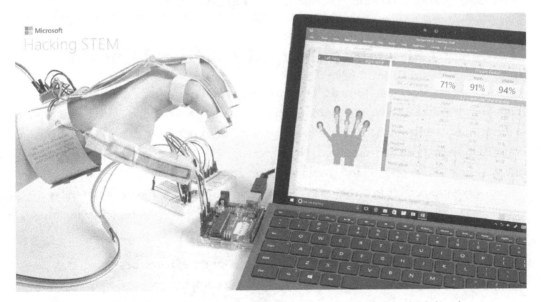

Figure 4.1　A sensorized glove captures motion data, which is used to control a robotic hand.

In addition to robotics, Microsoft's Hacking STEM website has a wealth of free resources, lesson plans, easy-to-follow step-by-step guides, and inexpensive options for getting started or taking your STEM learning to a new level.

- Explore Hacking STEM's lesson plans and resource guides. They even have projects for Lego and Hot Wheels: **tinyurl.com/y8q964fn**.

- For more Lego robotics courses, visit the Microsoft Educator Community and take free online courses in Mindstorm EV3 robotics: **tinyurl.com/y8qdkxss**.

- See examples of Mindstorm EV3 in action with Renton Prep students: **sway.com/5IAtYK2xXvT2UWPq**.

There are many free resources for computer science education, including lesson plans, step-by-step guides, and projects you can do as a class or as part of differentiated instruction.

- Microsoft Make Code: **makecode.com**
- Code.org: **code.org**
- Code Combat: **codecombat.com**
- Minecraft Education Edition Code Builder: **tinyurl.com/y8ynrb7e**
- Scratch by MIT: **scratch.mit.edu**
- Google for Education Blocky: **developers.google.com/blockly**

Diversity and Gender Equity in STEM Careers

As we consider the sociocultural aspects of learning and prepare for a future in which more humans interact with intelligent machines, we need to continually include diversity in the equation. Often, when we speak of diversity, we forget to include the voices of young people in those conversations. I have asked young people to represent throughout this book. I have asked them what they want educators to know. They understand the power of their voices from being in my class, presenting with me at conferences, speaking to industry professionals, writing for publications, or entering and winning competitions. They immediately agreed to add their voices to the discussion.

Without diversity at a very basic level, it will be hard for developers, designers, and creators to identify biases as they are creating AI, or the components of cognitive systems, robotics, and machine learning. In the first chapter, you read about examples of how accessibility tools are leveraging developing AI technologies, with motion sensors reading hand gestures to translate sign language, and tools that assist visually impaired users. Although this section of the chapter cannot cover the full range of diversities, it will highlight several with the goal of thinking more deeply about small details that may have big impact on representation.

According to Dr. Jamila Simpson, "We can't underestimate how important it is to see reflections of yourself." Simpson is an advocate for diversity in STEM. She graduated as the first African American woman to receive a B.S. in meteorology at North Carolina State University (Jones, 2017) and is the assistant dean for academic programs, student diversity, and engagement for the College of Sciences. She coordinated a STEM symposium to reach a diverse range of groups. In an online article for *Technician*, she described the importance of people being able to imagine themselves in a future career by seeing role models, or reflections of themselves: "I've had little kids and adults close their eyes and imagine a scientist doing science, and they usually imagine an older white male with crazy hair. They do not imagine themselves. If people can't see themselves in these roles, it creates a barrier" (Chappell 2018).

STEM IS FOR EVERYONE

Recall Mia Britt from the last chapter. She wrote a poem about diversity in the blog post, "Do not prove them right, prove them wrong: Student Voices Talking About Equity in Education and their Vision for Participating in Technology" (**tinyurl.com/y9vzfes8**). In a recent conversation with Mia, I asked what she wanted educators to know about diversity in STEM. Here is what she wrote:

Even in everyday life, it is important to be accepting and respectful of all cultures. Teach your students the importance of cultural diversity, encourage them to be respectful, and help them understand that STEM is for everyone. As technology grows at a rapid rate, there will be a higher demand for individuals to pursue STEM (Science, Technology, Engineering, Math) careers. People from all walks of life should be able to apply for these jobs, no matter where they have come from. STEM should not be something that is exclusively for those who have the opportunity to use the latest and greatest technology. When you have a large diversity of people coming from different cultures, ethnicities, gender identities, social classes, etc., there is no limit to what can be accomplished. More problems can be solved because when there is a larger range of people, there are more problems to be identified and more solutions to be thought of, while reducing bias. When every culture/gender is represented and respected in STEM, more people will feel comfortable to experiment and join the workforce, which can ultimately help further the development of technology. (Mia Britt, personal communication, May 1, 2018)

Figure 4.2
Students ages 12 though 15 mentor four-year-olds during a STEM challenge to create a structure that can support the weight of an apple using limited materials.

See what it can look like when older students mentor younger students in this 30-second video clip: **youtu.be/3F_AncTpFPw**.

Xoliswa Zinzile Mahlangu is from Soweto, Gauteng, South Africa. She is a computing curriculum developer and technology integration specialist with the Joburg Centre for Software Engineering (JCSE) at Wits University. I had the opportunity to meet her in Singapore for the Global Educator Exchange in March 2018. She has been doing incredible work to inspire girls in STEM, so I asked her to share her views on getting girls into STEM careers. Here is what she said:

Start them young. The girls who thrive in tech have been brought up with the belief that tech is also for them. It is the girls that have the chance to play with Lego and remote-controlled cars. It is the girls that were encouraged to do puzzles, play board games, and given the chance to make mistakes and not always expected to be "pretty little girls." With the intervention programs I have run, I have always said that I have mixed gender groups working on building tech solutions and have made it compulsory for everyone to work on coding parts of the solution. I have seen girls rising and shining above the boys when they get how the tech works. I have also challenged myself to not be afraid of new technology, but to embrace it and try new things all the time. The girls that I teach have seen this, and my courage and curiosity has become contagious. In this world of teaching to digital natives, I have learned that the students might sometimes know more than I do, and I equally call upon both boys and girls to assist me and the class in certain tasks. (X. Z. Mahlangu, personal communication)

The ImpaCT Programme was developed to help increase awareness of the ICT space. The 2017 focus was on building games for good—games that solve social issues with the African continent in mind. Xoliswa wanted students began design thinking with empathy to solve issues that plague them in everyday existence.

ImpaCT student Zanele Ngcobo talked about the social issue she wanted to address. She noticed people were forgetting where they come from and not keeping in touch with their roots. Japan and South Africa may seem very different in many respects, but in both locations, we see a human desire to know who you are, know more about your culture and how to honor the past while using new technologies to strengthen what some people may have lost sight of. Zanele's team won three awards. Watch her talk about her experience with ImpaCT here: **youtu.be/slecnhdh4al**.

JCSE WOMEN IN IT

Listen to Xoliswa talk about gender equality with JCSE Women in IT: **youtu.be/Z612oFLGOIo**.

REFLECTING ON DIVERSITY IN STEM CAREERS

- Discuss the ways the students discussed in this chapter told a story and how they represented diversity and equity.
- What is the value of including a poem and two videos that do not seem directly related to STEM careers in a section on Equity in STEM?

- How and why is this an important foundation for equity in STEM careers?

- Consider how each of the videos and poems demonstrate evidence of these students becoming:

  - Empowered learners
  - Digital citizens
  - Knowledge constructors
  - Innovative designers

  - Computational thinkers
  - Creative communicators
  - Global collaborators

Amanda Damman is Engineering Business Manager at General Motors. Here she shares her perspective on AI and gender equality in STEM fields.

ON AI AND GENDER EQUALITY

THE MOST URGENT NEED

While the systems we create and the technologies we use are rapidly evolving, there are foundational AI principles that will endure the test of time. Professionals working in this space will need to be willing to adapt and change at the same pace. It is, after all, the human brain that facilitates each technological advance we encounter. This commitment and flexibility will drive the industry and ultimately humanity forward.

The automotive industry has demonstrated a willingness to evolve at the required pace as it has embraced artificial intelligence to pursue the development of autonomous vehicles. Born from the software-minded Silicon Valley and manufacturing know-how from Detroit, teams are working together to change the face of the automotive industry. The effective combination of human intelligence and groundbreaking software has introduced us to self-driving vehicles. This development is the result of various systems including perception, behavioral control, mapping, controls, and simulation. Motivated by a vision of a world free of vehicle crashes, improved utilization of time spent commuting, and preserved independence of those unable to drive, the automotive industry, like many others, is poised to experience more change in the next five years than it has in the past 50.

ON GENDER EQUALITY

A rapid upsurge in artificial intelligence has increased the daily presence of technology in our lives. From voice recognition to mapping applications, suggestive searches to self-driving cars, AI is positively impacting the lives of people everywhere. While the benefits exist for both men and women, the same gender equality is not present in the industry driving this evolution. The tech industry and STEM fields continue to be dominated by men. There are contributing factors for this trend, including the sense that STEM fields may be more attractive to boys and men, girls losing interest in STEM as early as middle school, and some women perceiving STEM careers as masculine.

Women may use AI differently than men, and as we engineer self-driving vehicles, personal security is at the forefront. Women may see themselves benefiting from autonomous vehicles as they are accustomed to transporting children. Some carry different belongings in the vehicles and may have different expectations when it comes to usability and the overall experience. The gender gap that exists in the humans behind artificial intelligence cannot be ignored, as AI has the power to benefit men and women alike. Educators play a vital role in recognizing the critical need for gender equality in STEM careers and encouraging diversity within this rapidly evolving field.

HAIR AND DIVERSITY IN STEM CAREERS

Unintentional bias can easily slip into a design if someone isn't there to point it out. For example, Nile Wilson mentioned the challenge of collecting data that represents a range of people for something as simple as equipment that does not work well with certain hair types. It is easy to overlook hair as a factor in collecting data that could train a machine. As we will see next, it is also easy to miss how challenging it is to model hair in computer animation—most people do not realize all of the physics and math involved in creating art that responds naturally and tells a story. Pixar in a Box has been rising to the challenge by representing diversity and considering who young people see in various roles throughout the courses. In this example, I chose to highlight "Hair Simulation" because Pixar did not choose to represent the hair challenge as a problem to solve, but an important way to use math and physics to tell a character's story. The narrative in the introductory video conveys the perspective of a female software engineer stating that, "Hair was a really big deal in *Brave*. It was a symbol of freedom that was intrinsic to our main character's personality." In that small statement, Pixar has chosen to acknowledge the cultural importance of hair while demonstrating how physics, mathematics, software engineering, and coding play an important role in representation. Representing hair was worth the effort even though it "was hard. It took a lot of iterations to get it right. . . Merida feels like a real girl, messy, wild, and free."

HAIR SIMULATION ·

Explore an introductory video on hair simulation: **tinyurl.com/y77vdny9**.

· ·

In the book, *Hair Matters: Beauty, Power and Black Women's Consciousness,* Ingrid Banks (2000) writes:

Black women share a collective consciousness about hair, though it is articulated in a variety of ways. The first question I asked the girls and women is how and why hair matters. Given the many personal reflective writings by black women about their hair, I wanted the girls and women to explain if hair is important to them, too, or if the attention it gets is a lot of hype. The responses varied, but most of the women agreed that hair matters in some way to them in particular or to black women in general. (p. 21)

Hair may not be the first thing that comes to mind about when you think about diversity and STEM, but it illustrates the importance of representation in relation to emerging AI technologies. Historically, hair has played a role in representation across the globe (Banks, 2000; Ellery, 2014; *The Mercury*, 2016). For Pixar, the thoughtful use of hair to tell a story was a way of honoring individual identity. As we move forward with AI, it is vital to keep in mind all of the different ways diversity can impact—and be impacted by—the technology we create.

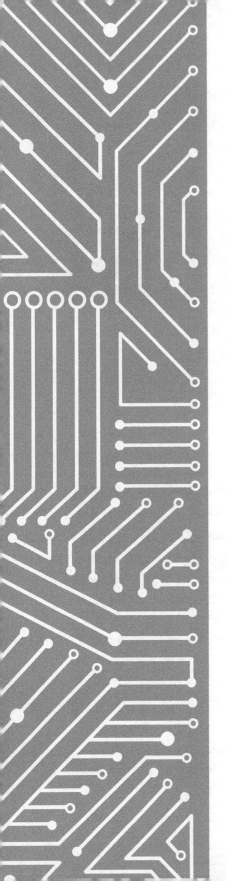

CHAPTER 5
How AI Can Support Teachers

Work Smarter, Not Harder

DRAMATIS PERSONAE

DAVID KELLERMANN: Lecturer in School of Mechanical and Manufacturing Engineering, University of New South Wales (UNSW), Sydney

T.A.: Human teacher's assistant

QUESTION BOT: Artificially intelligent teacher's assistant

STUDENTS: Introduction to Mechanical Engineering students

SCENE

University of New South Wales, Sydney, is an Australian public research university established in 1949 (Figure 5.1). It is ranked first in New South Wales, third in Australia, and 45th in the world, according to the 2017 QS World University Rankings.

TIME: April 2018

Figure 5.1
University of New
South Wales in Sydney,
Australia.

ACT II

Scene 5

SETTING: Introductory mechanical engineering class of 500 students—350 in person, and 150 joining online.

AT RISE: As 500 students study for their final exam, the online forums are abuzz with questions day and night. Kellermann, his teaching assistant, and his tutors work hard to answer as many questions as possible. Wonderfully, the students are also answering each other's questions. But in the fire hose of inquiries, questions still go unanswered. Tutors don't know who should answer whom, and they often spend time answering questions that have already been resolved, or whose answers can be found in the lecture recordings or course materials. Worst of all, at the end of semester, the forum will close and all the valuable dialogue will be lost in preparation for a new semester.

A week later, the stack of mechanical engineering final exams is overwhelming, to say the least. Imagine an exam 24 pages long, and multiply that by 500 students. That's 12,000 pages that need to be taken home to grade. The exams arrive in six enormous bags, carried slung over the T.A.'s shoulder. Imagine the mastery of physics required to move those inertial pages from one location to another without upsetting the stack—or the students. There are many tripping hazards between the lecture hall and the T.A.'s car. Worse yet, each exam paper must be passed along to 12 different graders, each of whom must evaluate all 500 answers to a given question—a task that requires them to leaf through the booklets to find the question they are grading. Finally, there is the day-long process of data entry. It all amounts to a mind-numbing exercise in logistics.

ACTION: Things are running differently this semester. Kellermann has designed, developed, and deployed a bot named *Question*, which students tag in the forum. Each topic from the syllabus has its own channel, so the bot knows which topic each question regards as well as who asked the question. Based on enrollment data, it also knows which tutorial class the student is in and who the tutors for that class are. Upon receiving a query, *Question* sends push notifications to the phone and PC of the two tutors responsible for the student. The bot also keeps track of the question's status, providing a button to click once it has been answered. If a fellow student answers it first, the push notifications are canceled. The system allows tutors to keep track of all unanswered questions posed by their 40 students. Whenever someone answers a question, the bot adds the Q&A to its knowledge database, which is sorted by topic. In Figure 5.2, the tutor can click the "Answered" button once the question has been resolved. This signals the bot to file the information within the appropriate syllabus topic—"Energy methods," indicated by the channel.

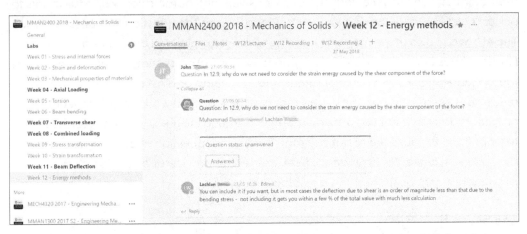

Figure 5.2 As students' questions are answered, the bot adds each correct response to its knowledge base, which it can draw upon to answer similar questions in the future.

Not only does the bot serve as an invaluable study resource for students, but it can also use its natural language processing APIs to understand questions similar to those asked earlier in the semester—or, eventually, even those posed in previous years. It has already started to harness the collective knowledge of the lecturer, the T.A., 12 tutors, and the students themselves. Moreover, yet another AI tool has automatically generated closed captions for the lecture recording, and the *Question* bot is able to determine if the student's question has already been answered in the lecture transcript. If it has a confident match, the bot provides a deep link directly to the exact moment in the lecture where the answer lies, and the video begins to play. The tutors' workload is reduced as the bot starts to take care of the easier questions, allowing them to focus on the difficult ones. Their ability to add deep human insight to the conversation has been leveraged.

Come exam time, the 12,000 pages of exams are fed into an automatic scan feeder. An AI bot reads the student number from every front page and separates each question into a two-page PDF. Each lot of 500 questions is batch uploaded to the cloud, and grading tasks are assigned to the tutors, who are ready to go with a rubric and touch buttons. They will assign marks directly to the spreadsheet. The bags full of exams are gone. The round robin of booklets is gone. The hundreds of hours spent leafing through pages to find the right questions are gone, as are the hours of laborious data entry. The tutors can grade exams anywhere, with nothing more than a laptop or tablet, and they can even provide feedback using digital ink. But the AI bot is not done assisting with digitized exams. It can read the final numerical answers and automatically give full marks to perfect calculations. If the final answer is wrong, it flags the question for human review. The AI bot can also utilize machine learning to mark graphs and diagrams that are correct—it has been trained using the graded exams from last semester. It can also parse the language of the written explanations and map them against a sample of acceptable responses. All this has immensely reduced the logistical workload of the lecturer and tutors, freeing them up to spend more time writing insightful feedback for students to learn from. Because the AI bot can map every exam question to every topic, every conversation, and every attendance item, it is able to provide analytical feedback on an individual student basis. And this is just the beginning.

End Scene 5

Automating Tasks to Free Up Educator Time

In a visit to UNSW, Sydney, in April 2018, I spoke with David Kellermann about how AI supports him as an educator at the School of Mechanical and Manufacturing Engineering. He gave a vivid description of stacks of papers; in pre-university settings, not many of us end up with 12,000 pages to grade at the end of a term, but that visual can evoke a great deal of empathy in any educator who has had to haul and grade a huge stack of papers.

It may be of interest to note here that in the design thinking (DT) process, empathy is the first step on the path to innovation. In Kellermann's class, for example, there are not enough seats at the university to physically accommodate everyone, leaving some students to take the course online. He noticed a discrepancy between students who took his course in person, and those who listened to online recordings of his lectures. So he set out to discover why.

Human Aspects of Sociocultural Learning That Make a Difference

Kellermann determined that nonverbal communication, visual aids, and participation in face-to-face class discussions were contributing to the gap. He had discovered a clear learning disparity between those who engaged in the social process of learning and those who learned directly from a machine, in isolation from others. He wanted a more equitable solution, even if not everyone could attend in person. During our conversation, he asserted that massive open online courses (MOOCs) and flipped classrooms can kill engagement and feedback, removing collaboration and communication from the learning process and leaving some students with an impoverished experience. Introductory mechanical engineering can be a challenging course, he said, and students need the sociocultural aspects of learning.

In a case like this, an educator alone cannot balance the load without personal knowledge of the nuances in students' struggles and gaps. Kellermann found, however, that when students used their real photos as profile images in Microsoft Teams—and when they began interacting online to answer each other's questions—they were able to instantly connect upon seeing each other in person. Some educators may have experienced a similar phenomenon when they've met someone in person at a conference after following them on social media or seeing their work online. Digital interaction seems to help people forge a deeper and more immediate connection in person, allowing them to initiate conversations more quickly compared to educators who have never communicated though technology prior to meeting in person.

Since moving to Microsoft Teams, Kellermann has seen an 800% increase in discussion posts. At the conclusion of his course, 100% of the students who participated from a distance reported in their student experience surveys that they "felt part of the learning community." Their learning community became anchored in Microsoft Teams.

While technology can remove human interaction from the learning equation, leaving students deprived, it can also provide tools that help support the sociocultural aspects of learning. Through platforms such as Microsoft Teams, machine learning has the computing power to assist educators in identifying areas that need support, notifying humans when intervention is required, and facilitating socially mediated learning (Vygotsky, 1987). In the example at the beginning of the chapter, Kellermann used technology to augment human connection. Contrast that with the scene from the animated film *WALL-E*, in which technology supplanted human communication. When a tool can help educators build community, student engagement increases.

COLLABORATE USING MICROSOFT TEAMS · · · · · · · · · · · · · · · · · ·

Microsoft Teams is a digital hub for educators and students. It allows users to collaborate around classes and assignments, connect in professional learning communities, and communicate with one another.

Learn more or get started at **tiny.cc/1b6r0y**.

· ·

Data Mining

Schools collect a massive volume of assessment and performance data, which can reveal trends and patterns in student progress—valuable information educators can use to improve teaching and learning. But the data remains fallow if no one has the time or expertise to analyze it. Fortunately, AI has stepped up to fill in the gap. **Data mining**, an interdisciplinary subfield of computer science, is the computational process of discovering patterns in large data sets using methods that stem from the intersection of artificial intelligence, machine learning, statistics, and database systems (Wikipedia, n.d.).

Educators are increasingly using data mining to process and deliver student performance data to teachers, allowing them to more easily spot struggling learners who need extra help (Haigh, 2007).

Assessment

In Kellermann's course, data mining had a measurable impact on student success. Exam pass rates for the class using Microsoft Teams increased from 65% to 85%. As part of his data mining efforts, he wanted to move beyond multiple choice tests and basic responses to find out whether his students understood the material and were able to apply the knowledge. That required the ability to demonstrate understanding in a more fluid way, including through drawings with digital ink. This posed a challenge for automating assessment. Figures 5.3 and 5.4 are examples of real student work from a sample assessment.

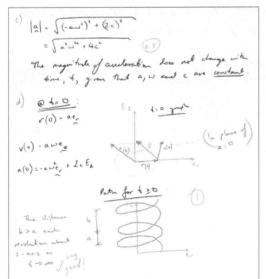

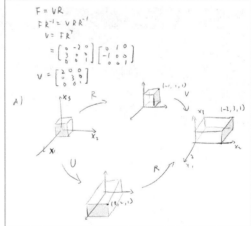

Figure 5.3   Student example done in digital ink.

Figure 5.4   Student example done in digital ink.

To assess this type of work, Kellermann needed more complex machine assistance. He identified four categories of response types and matched them with the corresponding marking technology needed to assess student work:

1. Yes/no, multiple choice, or numerical: *Boolean*

2. Written answers: *O.C.R., natural language processing, and AI*

3. Graphs and diagrams: *Machine learning for positives*

4. Mathematical reasoning: *Humans when flagged for review*

In addition to processing multiple choice and "yes" or "no" answers, assessments can now incorporate machine learning, natural language processing and computer vision, and human judgment. With machine learning for positives, the AI only gives positive marks. If the computer identifies all components of a problem as correct, including written ones, the item is marked as correct. When there is a discrepancy, the machine flags a human to review the answer and use their judgment to understand where the student went wrong. With every answer, the machine continues to learn. This has reduced the job down to 20% of what it used to be by automating everything except the flagged items. It scrapes away all of the repetitive work, allowing educators to focus on the rich, human part of assessment—to look at the nuances.

Throughout the course, educators are now able to pull assessment data into Power BI, an analytics service provided by Microsoft, and display it in students' personal sections in OneNote (shown in Figure 5.5) so they can visually see their progress.

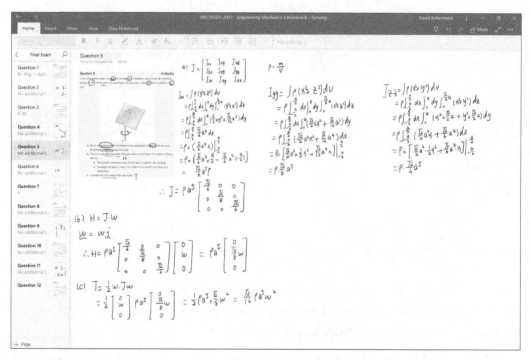

Figure 5.5 An example of a structured final exam in engineering, using digital ink with real-time synchronization in OneNote.

Success Supported by Augmentation from AI, Machine Learning, and Human Interaction

After deploying AI, Kellermann's survey results indicated that his first-year mechanical engineering students felt successful, connected, and part of a community. The responses were unprecedented—a stark contrast to previous survey results, as well as the results of other mechanical engineering courses in which this method is not yet in use. Kellermann has identified what made this application of AI different:

> *Looking back, we can see that the use of AI was not about convenience—such as the way a digital assistant can save you 10 seconds by giving you the weather, or setting a reminder or alarm. It was also not about saving money in educational delivery. The AI enabled insight to be leveraged in different ways, such that each of those 500 students gained more from their educational experience. (D. Kellermann, personal communication, and 2018)*

Beyond the technology, beyond the human connection between students, perhaps the most compelling part of Kellermann's story is his desire to provide early intervention for students who may be struggling. Machine learning has helped him with early detection, allowing him to predict the likelihood that students will continue to struggle—or even drop the course. Because he was able to identify these cases earlier, and because the chatbot fielded all of the student questions that had already been addressed in the course content, he was able to devote his time to interventions that could change a student's trajectory and support continued learning in STEM career fields.

AI, and specifically machine learning, can also highlight specific areas where students consistently show strength, giving educators the opportunity to suggest electives, highlight natural aptitudes, and recommend skills matches earlier. It can help identify particularly rare combinations of skills that organizations will highly prize in future employment—skills that may otherwise get lost in a numerical grade or percentage. Some employers miss out on that perfect match because tests highlight only one aspect of a job candidate's learning while areas where the student shines can't be easily demonstrated. This can cause frustration for students, who may end up changing majors or even choosing an entirely new career path. The world needs talents and skills that aren't clearly demonstrated through test scores—especially as we work to define what humans can contribute in a world where machines can excel at the same skills our assessments were created to measure.

Beyond these grading and assessment examples, AI and machine learning have provided Kellermann with a single hub for students, simplifying class administration. He can now quickly push a meeting, assignment, or exam date to all students from within their own Outlook calendars. Lecture notes are synchronized in OneNote. Videos are available through Microsoft Stream, and chatbots can direct students to the precise section of the video that holds the answer to their question. These technologies working together have revolutionized both this instructor's experience and that of his students.

Working Out a Roadmap for Smarter, Not Harder

Creating an AI-driven system like Kellermann's requires pulling together multiple AI tools into one framework. In a conversation with LeiLani Cauthen, CEO of The Learning Counsel and author of *The Consumerization of Learning: How educators can co-opt consumer-grade digital courseware to transform learning in the Age of Experience*, I asked her what she wanted educators to know about AI and how she imagined it could support them. This is what she had to say:

> *AI in the realm of education is going in the direction of recommendations engines for lessons, for remediation, for tangential content, and for personalized pathways. Inside adaptive courseware and resource collections websites is one area where AI is forming with complex algorithms. It's there that the burden is shifted from search-and-deploy manually in framework systems to more of an automatic deployment with feedback analytics and leveraging for teachers. The biggest hurdle is the disparate subject-focused systems, and working out a roadmap to tie together those pieces into one curriculum map with a multiplicity of directionality for personalization. (L. Cauthen, personal communication, May 4, 2018)*

Although pieces exist and advancements have been made, individual educators must still put in a lot of work to find, vet, and combine AI tools to produce a working system that helps teachers work smarter, not harder. As people like Kellermann refine their systems and abstract the framework to facilitate the transfer from university level to K–12 classrooms, incorporating AI will become easier—but there are limitations for replicating a structure such as Kellermann's in a K–12 setting. Elementary school teachers typically teach most or all subjects, and while that type of scaling is possible, the technology just isn't there yet. Machines also need vast amounts of training data before they can help assess exams with images and words. UNSW has 500 students in one term, but smaller classes would take longer to produce enough iterations to train the machine. However, as we saw from some of the work Google is doing with imagery, there have been strides in the ability of a machine to recognize or predict drawings.

Arts, Music, and AI

We've seen many examples of how AI can facilitate student learning. Programs like ALEKS support mathematics teachers in assessing and correctly identifying gaps in understanding. Programs like Mia Learning can assist educators in differentiating reading instruction and gaining a better understanding of their students' progress. OneNote Learning Tools not only offer accessibility features but also help students in typically developing classrooms with listening, revising, reading, and comprehension. But what can machine learning do to support educators in teaching arts like drawing and music?

MIXING TOOLS FOR MUSIC CLASS

At Northwest Council for Computer Educators (NCCE) in February 2018, I had the opportunity to speak with Andrew Fitzgerald, instrumental music teacher at Franklin Classical Middle School in Long Beach, California. Although he did not specify AI, he uses a range of tools—including Kahoot!, Go Formative, Socrative, Office Forms, and the Office business analytics tool Power BI—to become more efficient and help his students understand their own progress as they pursue their learning goals (Figure 5.6). In an article for the Microsoft Education blog, he described how he uses a mix of tools to more effectively assess student growth.

> *Assessing the individual performance of my music students is a time-consuming process, especially with a class of 50+ students. . . I assess every student—and their classmates provide feedback when they perform. We use an Office Form in which to enter scores and constructive feedback for each student. . . By importing my data into Power BI, I can organize scores and feedback specific to my instrument sections and individual students, easily share it with them, and use this data for personal reflection and growth mindset–related activities. (A. Fitzgerald, personal communication, February, 2018)*

Learn more and see examples of how Fitzgerald organizes student assessment data at **tiny.cc/gasbxy** and on his blog, **andrewfitz.net**.

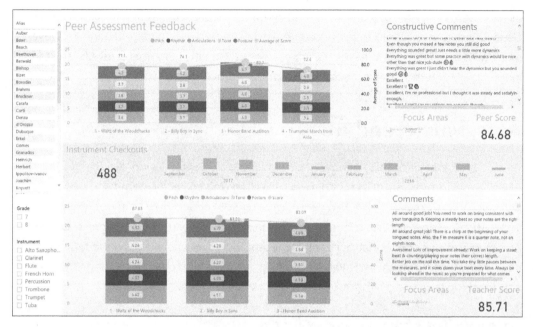

Figure 5.6 Digital tools assist with both teacher and peer assessment of instrumental music skills.

PORTFOLIO TOOLS FOR ART ASSESSMENT

AI can support traditional art assessment with portfolio tools that simplify the process of student reflection, providing an easier way for educators to track works in progress. Using a machine learning algorithm to optimize aesthetics for their final presentation, students can focus their time and effort on creating the artwork rather than on designing their portfolios. Although art teachers may not take home thousands of pages to grade at the end of the term, art courses in traditional mediums pose a challenge when it comes to keeping and scoring the final products. Such works either take up a lot of space in the classroom, or students must carry large portfolios to transport their work.

Tools like Office Lens can take photos with a mobile device and remove parallax for a more polished presentation. As shown in Figure 5.7, having students document their progress in completing graphite grid pictures provides a level of self-reflection and peer-assessment; and an artifact to submit, keep, and share on social media—or even their LinkedIn profiles. Because projects of this complexity are an important part of STEAM learning, this format allows for a more complex review of content and better communication with families so they might understand the significance of students' artwork.

—
Conclusion and Reflection

Grid pictures were never easy but over the years I have learned plenty of techniques that could help me do it on my own. Practice, failing and re-drafting is always going to happen whether or not you have done it one time or for the twentieth time. Looking at the smallest details of either your hair or hands and trying to replicate something so real onto a piece of paper and getting it right, is a very satisfying feeling. Shapes and measurements are a huge part of this project, as I have learned over the years, and looking at what you see is different then what you think. Even though this is a challenge every time I do it, there is a very satisfying feeling when you see your work and how similar it is to a photograph, which just amazes me.

Figure 5.7   A student uses Sway to reflect on the process of drawing graphite grid pictures.

STUDENT EXAMPLES IN SWAY ·

Explore examples of students reflecting on their art progress in Sway:

- Myra Tso's Grid Picture Progress by Myra Tso:
  sway.com/0sO7CNLVWIhhGPIJ?ref=Link&loc=mysways

- The Story Behind My Gift by Sharice Lee:
  sway.office.com/AbARTZpfM5VtW6vR?ref=Link

- Red Dot Fuji by Afomeya Hailu:
  sway.office.com/3O1bo95AOvEgJJ1f?ref=Link

- The Story Behind My Gift by Emmy Sung:
  sway.office.com/D8oCdEZjcWDsB3sP?ref=Link

Apprenticeship in the Digital Age

The added benefit of an assessment method that captures progress, rather than just assessing the finished product, is that others can gain insight into the student's process. Educators can model assignments based on what they see, while students can learn from others who have completed the work in advance. The ability to learn from another person's process is the basis for apprenticeship, a time-honored learning technique. While that type of one-on-one support and guidance is not possible for an individual teacher with a large classroom, AI can help fill the gap. As repetitive and basic tasks are increasingly performed by machines, humans can move more toward apprenticeship models of learning with higher levels of human interaction. This aligns with the high-touch and high-tech model.

The apprenticeship model (Rogoff, 1991) describes the relationship between a novice and a more experienced expert, who guides the novice through hands-on involvement in a shared activity. The expert decides how to divide the activity into smaller subgoals on a scale the apprentice can handle, while also providing helpful advice on how to apply the tools (Cole, 1989) and skills required (Rogoff, 1991). Jonathan Grudin, design researcher at Microsoft, touched on the value of apprenticeship when discussing whether AI will replace educators:

> What I would want to tell educators would depend on whether they were teaching about what AI is, how the world will be with a relatively conservative prediction of AI plus other technologies, or how they can or will use AI in doing their work. I would lean on the augmentation or supplement side. I would say that as far as education goes, people are wired to learn by apprenticeship as we did for millions of years, from other people, and that won't change. No technology will replace a good, insightful, empathic, inspiring teacher, but it can help the teacher and sometimes be available when the teacher can't be. (J. Grudin, personal communication, 2018)

From a sociocultural perspective, teaching and learning is about more than just a brain and a body. There are complex processes that happen in the presence of others, including the development of empathy and ethics.

AI for Augmentation to Support Educators

We have learned from research that motivation can be crucial in learning (Ryan & Deci, 2000). When asked about the role of AI in education at Alan November's Building Learning Communities conference in Boston in July 2017, Zoran Popovic, University of Washington professor, director of the Center for Game Sciences, and founder of Enlearn, replied that when they trained machines to prompt educators to physically give students a high-five hand gesture, rather than delivering a reward on the screen, students performed better. Human teacher input matters. Harnessing data and collecting artifacts is one thing. How we use them to support and encourage student learning is another.

One way both educators and those experienced in AI can work across disciplines is to help identify goals for future generations. Motivation to persist when things get difficult (Ryan & Deci, 2000) is crucial for more than just academics. What Grudin says makes sense alongside empirical research findings. Humans have innate psychological needs, including the need for relational connection, a sense of choice, and a feeling of success. In Ryan and Deci's (2000) work, they refer to this as "relatedness, autonomy, and competence." When those three innate psychological needs are met, people are more likely to persist when things get difficult. It makes sense that AI would help boost autonomy and competence, but a human connection is needed to build a sense of relatedness. We see this happening in mentoring with both older and younger children, as well as in in success stories across the globe.

What Teachers Can Add to AI Augmentation

The image in Figure 5.8 is of a real student dashboard within ALEKS, described on the website (**aleks.com/about_aleks**) as "a Web-based, artificially intelligent assessment and learning system." She is a motivated student who appreciates being able to excel in academic content. Using her dashboard, she can identify a clear goal and see the outcomes of her progress. For some students, this is motivating; others, however, may feel defeated and shut down. According to Grudin, "Some kids will respond well if the system gives them increasingly difficult problems until they get one they can't do. Other kids will feel deflated if every problem session ends with a failure. Teachers can get insight into motivational differences that these systems don't have time or ability to pick up. AI can help them; but it won't replace them" (2018).

Educators have the capacity to learn the nuances of a student's behavior and determine how to motivate them differently. That is where the power of ML comes in, identifying when human connection is needed and prompting an educator to step in—combining high-touch with high-tech. Even in an apprenticeship for mathematics, it would be difficult for a human to know all aspects of mathematics mastery and pinpoint gaps in understanding. This is where AI excels.

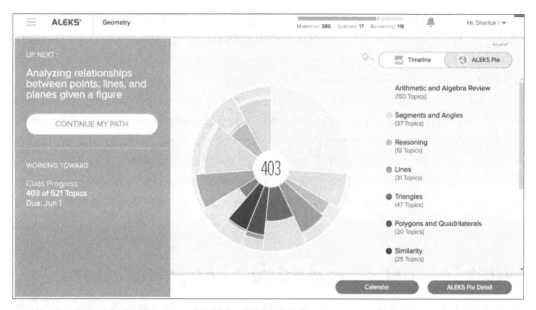

Figure 5.8 A dashboard displays a student's progress through the ALEKS mathematics courses.

Students who complete ALEKS mathematics courses, for example, can track their own progress via a dashboard, which defines progress to completion and the breakdown of core concepts that comprise that particular math course. In Figure 5.8, the amount of color filled in demonstrates the amount of mastery achieved in that learning path. On the left, the adaptive program offers recommendations for the student's learning path. The progress bar on the top shows how much of the course has been mastered and how much remains. This program is used in colleges to assess math level and gaps as well as to better adapt to student pace and progress.

REFLECTING ON AI ·

- What are ways you imagine AI can support you as an educator?

- What ways do you imagine may be possible in the future based on what you have learned?

- In what ways do you have the capability to excel at supporting students where machines are not effective?

- What do you think about using facial recognition in classrooms to identify emotions or behaviors?

- What does it mean to work smarter, not harder?

The Importance of Teachers: Physical Education as an Example of AI Augmentation

Motivation does not end with mathematics, engineering, or the fine arts. Physical education is another area where educators may begin using AI to support learning. In the sports industry, AI is being used to analyze performance, human biomechanics, and health data to offer coaching support for performance and training (SportTechie, 2018).

Seismic (**myseismic.com**) is addressing human biomechanics to optimize performance, tracking body movements in real time with MotionScience Platform (**tinyurl.com/yalqm6jj**). Data is already supporting the use of AI in wearable technology designed to improve posture (Lumo Lift), while a coaching platform for runners (Lumo Run) has proven effective at helping runners perform more efficiently and improve their run times (Bradley, 2017).

While AI will continue to advance, giving rise to more wearable technology designed to support athletics and sports training, educators and coaches will remain important. Grudin made this point in a conversation on May 5, 2018:

> My example is from my first paid job as a tennis instructor. It seemed like what we did was teach how to hit each stroke. At the time, you could get instruction on how to hit each stroke from videocassettes, and later YouTube, but that didn't put tennis coaches out of work. What might AI do? Let's say it gets so awesomely good that it can identify every mistake a player is making from analyzing videos. (I doubt it can now, my guess is that it might suggest things to a coach who can look at the videos and do a better analysis, but let's say it can.) It can identify the eight mistakes that the student is making on forehand and backhand. It notifies the coach. Is the coach out of a job? No, the coach will size the student up and decide how motivated he or she is. It is unclear whether the student will react well or badly to hearing that there are eight problems with these strokes. Perhaps the coach will only mention three at first—decide which two to focus on now, and how hard to push the student before high-fiving and heading for the shower. As a tennis coach, I actually thought there were two crucial things: 1) to keep the player motivated and playing (my advice was, find someone you like to play with and play a lot), and 2) to teach them to serve correctly, as no one self-learns a good serve. I could help with the other shots, of course, but motivation was key. Recognition and machine learning systems won't be going there.

Developing Chatbots

Ashok Goel has referred to the simplified intersection of cognitive systems, robotics, and machine learning as parts of AI that are not yet integrated. He is also known for his work with Jill Watson, a chatbot that he created for his college course. His regular courses at Georgia Tech had at most a few dozen students, but his online students numbered 400 from all over the world. He fielded more than 10,000 questions in a semester—a load he and his staff couldn't feasibly handle. And, as we heard before, there is a discrepancy in learning between those who take a course in person and those who learn online. Educational researcher Katy Jordan has demonstrated that fewer than 15% of students actually complete MOOC courses after they've enrolled (**katyjordan.com**). Goel created Jill Watson, an intelligent tutor, while he was teaching a course on Knowledge-Based Artificial Intelligence. Although Jill Watson wasn't immediately effective and provided some strange answers, it became 97% effective at responding to basic questions. Just to begin training, though, he needed to upload four semesters' worth of data, which comprised 40,000 questions and answers, along with other chatter.

Goel told *Wired* magazine that Jill Watson isn't ready to teach or take on the responsibilities of a human T.A.: "We're not months away or years away. We're decades, maybe centuries away, at least in my estimation. None of us (AI experts) think we're going to build a virtual teacher for 100 years or more."

UNDERSTANDING AI

- Read more about Ashok Goel's work with Jill Watson in *Wired*: **wired.com/2016/12/a-secret-ops-ai-aims-to-save-education**.

- Read the research he wrote with Lalith Polepeddi on Jill Watson and AI applications for online education: **smartech.gatech.edu/handle/1853/59104**.

- Review the Crash Course video on natural language processing to learn more about chatbots and parsing answer trees: **youtu.be/fOvTtapxa9c**.

When Grudin worked on a chatbot project, he discovered that chatbots can be considerably more difficult than he had imagined. Marching a person through a question-and-answer tree, like a telephone answering system, is one thing; imbuing a bot with personality, on the other hand, is very difficult.

WORKING WITH CHATBOTS ·

While virtual teachers may be a long way from becoming a reality, you can create a chatbot with your students using existing tools. Chatbots—applications that perform one or more automated tasks using conversation as the interface—are used in a number of ways across the internet and on various devices. They provide services such as:

- **Information retrieval:** Lookup, reference, and information seeking. For example: "What subjects are offered for year 12 in 2018?" and "When are the trains leaving on Thursday?"

- **Transactional:** Look up information and make amendments. For example: "Upgrade my account to plan B" and "Book two tickets for film A on Monday using my credit card."

- **Advisory role:** Prescriptive guidance via "expert systems" based on user input. For example: "Are these school shoes appropriate?" and "Should I add another component to my service plan?"

- **Social conversations:** Sense sentiment and engage in open-ended conversation within the bot's area of expertise. For example: "Your product is terrible, I would like a refund." and "I have had a terrible experience, who can I talk to?" (Afshar, 2018)

Discuss with students the role chatbots play in our lives. Brainstorm other possible applications for chatbots and virtual assistants. Explore the following resources for building a chatbot:

- How to Build a Chatbot in 10 Minutes (**tinyurl.com/y6u3jofq**): Inspired by a workshop on Azure and Chatbots by Ray Fleming at the Microsoft Learning Partner Summit in January 2018, this blog walks you through the process of building a chatbot using a variety of tools.

- How to Build a Chatbot Without Coding (**tinyurl.com/y868ex8f**): This Coursera course using Watson natural language processing capabilities doesn't require coding knowledge.

- Build a Chatbot with IBM Watson APIs (**teamtreehouse.com/go/build-a-chatbot-with-watson-apis**): Treehouse has teamed up with IBM Watson to create this course, which shows you how to build a chatbot using natural language processing services available from IBM Watson and IBM Cloud Platform.

- Amazon Lex (**aws.amazon.com/lex**): Experiment with the same algorithms and technologies that power Amazon Alexa.

· ·

How Educators Around the World Are Considering Their Role in Educational AI

You may be wondering if schools are already replacing educators with AI, and how your school compares to others in preparing students for a future with AI. I asked a range of educators from different countries about their thoughts on AI. After the caution I received from researchers to not get swept up in the AI hype seen in headlines, I wanted to investigate more. After all, learning to ask questions is one of the proposed methods for preparing for a future with AI. I found myself making assumptions that countries with a lot of media headlines must surely be further ahead in the AI race than the U.S. The first educator I asked was Hidekazu Shoto in Japan. It was clear that his school was creating a solid learning foundation to prepare students for the future of technology.

HIDEKAZU SHOTO, JAPAN

Hidekazu Shoto is head of the ICT department and an English teacher at Ritsumeikan Primary. With as much media as I've seen about Japan being highly advanced in AI, I assumed that schools in the U.S. must be far behind Japan in the use of AI. I asked Shoto, "There is a lot of conversation on artificial intelligence and people asking if it will ever replace humans to teach children. What do people at your school think about this?" He responded, "We are facing this problem. Actually, to be honest, many teachers don't think too much. Japan is very behind other countries" (personal communication). I searched for other stories that may have provided more context and found an article from Japan Policy Forum that discussed artificial intelligence, the Japanese game Shogi, and how AI's success at the game helped shift attitudes toward AI in a positive direction (Mataki, 2016). From my research, and as a result of speaking with experts, Ritsumeikan Primary is elegantly preparing their students for a future that will implement AI in classrooms and also will continue to appreciate humanity while seeking effective ways technology can augment what we can do as teachers.

PHUTI RAGOPHALA, SOUTH AFRICA

Phuti Ragophala is a Varkey Teacher Ambassador from Seshego, Limpopo, South Africa. I met the former principal of Pula Madibogo Primary School at the Global Educator Exchange in Singapore in March 2018. She said she believes everyone is born with his or her intelligence. There may be variation in the level of intelligence, but now we live in environments and times where we have machine learning and AI as part of our daily lives. Still, she said, it shouldn't replace teachers. She added:

We need to empower, add up, and boost our level of intelligence through reading, learning, and teaching. And one of those tools to be used to learn is technology in order to adapt to the era where we are. To me, artificial intelligence works because if it was not for it, I would not have been where I am today. Living a natural life today is not enough. Yes, in the olden days maybe it was possible, but gone are those days where natural intelligence alone can serve a purpose in life. (P. Ragophala, personal communication, March 2018)

NAM THANH NGO, VIETNAM

A 2018 Global Teacher Prize Top 50 Finalist from Da Kao, Nam Thanh Ngo said machines may be able to replace teachers on the podium in the future, but teachers do not simply teach knowledge. Teaching is not the same as throwing out information and expecting others to remember it, like copying data to a hard drive, and it will never become an old-fashioned profession. Besides providing knowledge, it also requires insight and teaching methods that are appropriate for each subject. So far, there has been no sign that AI has the power to teach children spelling or arithmetic. He expects AI will help people work hard, but it cannot replace humans.

AGGELIKI PAPPA, GREECE

Aggeliki Pappa from Athens, Greece, is an ambassador at Varkey Teacher Foundation and an advocate for students with dyslexia. She weighed in on this topic, saying, "As all things in life, they become useful or dangerous according to the way we use them. The answer lies in our choices. Let's be wise and use technology for our common benefit, respecting all different parameters and dimensions."

Rather than fearing AI as a possible replacement, teachers can benefit from embracing the technology as a tool that enhances their ability to foster deeper learning. As machine learning and automation take over the more repetitive tasks associated with teaching, educators will have more time to focus on the human side of learning. Working side by side with AI, teachers can improve student outcomes while also modeling the types of human-machine collaborations students will encounter in their future jobs.

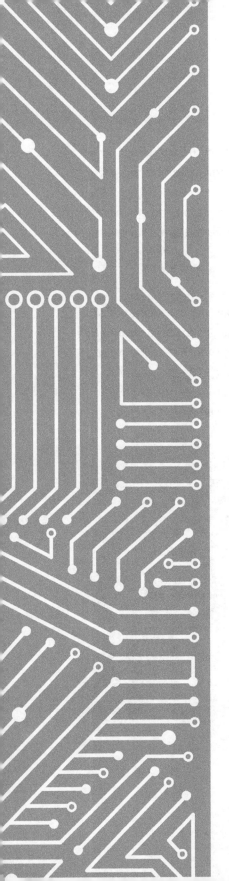

CHAPTER 6
Ethical Considerations

A Sick Baby and the Boy Who Did Not Hide Behind a Newspaper

DRAMATIS PERSONAE

ALGERNON HERRIES: Headmaster of a boys' school in England

PETHERICK: A student from the school

CHUFF: A student from the school

MOTHER: A train passenger with a sick baby

BABY: A catalyst for action

SCENE

The headmaster is giving a short closing speech at his retirement celebration, during which he reminisces about memorable former students.

TIME: Spring, mid-1940s

ACT II

Scene 6

AT RISE: The headmaster of a boys' school in England is retiring from years of service. At the dinner celebration for his retirement, people offer congratulations and gifts. The headmaster responds with a short speech about the number of highly successful students he has supported and guided since 1904—though he refuses to claim credit for their academic success. He believes they would have achieved the same success at any institution, given the same materials. He concludes with a story that defines what he sees as success.

> **HEADMASTER:** . . . *But helping to equip two generations of predatory males with the qualities of patience, tolerance, good fellowship, and the ability to see someone else's point of view—qualities I see as the keystones of democracy—that's something else. I'll pipe down now—did I catch a gutsy sigh of relief from the back? But let me close with a final anecdote, one that came to mind when I was riffling through the Old Boys' register this morning, in search of inspiration from this interminable valediction.*

It was a very trivial incident, but it must have impressed me at the time. Why else should it have stayed in the mind for nearly 20 years? It concerned two boys, Petherick and 'Chuff' Rodgers, who accompanied me over to Barcombe by train, when we were giving a charity performance of that year's opera. It was Christmas time, and the train was very full. We finally secured seats in a compartment where a young woman was nursing a baby. Within minutes of starting out, the baby was dramatically sick . . . I remember poor Petherick's expression well, as he took refuge behind my copy of The Times. Upside down it was, but a thing like that wouldn't bother Petherick. He was one of our sky-rockets, and went on to become president of a famous insurance company, and collect the O.B.E, or whatever they give the cream of insurance brokers. But I wasn't thinking so much of Petherick but of Chuff. Always unlucky, he had been sitting on the receiving end of the business. I didn't know what to do, but Chuff did. He whipped out a handkerchief—the only clean handkerchief I'd ever seen him sport—leaned across, wiped the baby's face and then the mother's lap. And when I say 'wiped' I mean wiped. It wasn't a dab. It was more of a general tidy-up, all around. After that we had a tolerably uneventful journey, with Rodgers making soothing noises all the way to the junction.

Now some of you might think that this is a very damp squib to conclude the regular fireworks display we have had here tonight, with so many kind speeches, and the giving of such splendid farewell gifts, but it isn't, you know. It's very relevant, to me at any rate, relevant to what we've all been engaged in up here on the moor all these years. For Chuff Rodgers, bless his thick skull, never won a prize or a race in his life. Neither did he find time to do the only thing he was equipped to do—raise a family. He was killed at First Ypres, but I still remember him. Rather better than I remember Petherick. As a matter of fact, when I came across his name this morning, I thought of him as one of our outstanding successes. (Delderfield, 1972)

End Scene 6

The Human Side of AI

What does a story about a mother with a sick baby on a crowded train have to do with a chapter on ethical considerations regarding AI? In the historical novel *To Serve Them All My Days* (1972), about a private boys' school in England between 1918 and the mid-1940s, the retiring headmaster reflects on his career as an educator. The story he remembers 20 years later is one of a boy who cared enough to use his one clean handkerchief to help a mother and her sick baby. He did not avoid the messiness of life for the sake of self-preservation. He engaged by showing compassion. Imagine what the mother felt when someone cared enough to assist her. This student was one of the school's "out-standing successes"—not because he won awards or accolades, but because of what he offered as a human being, even if in a seemingly small way. Young people can achieve academic content knowledge through formal education, but this story reminds us that formal education should consist of more than just content. It should be about developing humans into productive citizens who leave the world a better place. This is especially important as they interact with powerful technologies like AI.

What do we want our young people to be able to do when they complete formal education?

Technology amplifies who we are as humans. As we have learned from the brief history of computing, protective laws lag behind technological innovation. If we allow AI to continue its rapid advancement without engaging in ethical discussions or creating enforceable policies, the new frontiers for learning can quickly become a reboot of the Wild West. Educators can help young people think about the impact of AI through discussions on digital citizenship, ethics, and philosophy. Having students create class policies and methods for enforcing them can also be a good first step. Watch these videos for examples of student-created policies: **tinyurl.com/y8rzo68x**.

This chapter addresses ethical considerations teachers need to be aware of as they explore AI with their students—including loss of control, loss of privacy, cyberbullying, and cyberattacks. Students need to engage in these discussions with adults, because it is their generation that will be impacted by the choices we make now.

Loss of Control

Imagine yourself on the train with the English headmaster and his students. This time, however, the brakes fail and the train careens toward disaster. You are near enough to a switch to redirect the train to another track. Would you do it to save everyone?

Now imagine there's a worker on the track who would not have time to move out of the way if the train was diverted. What would you do? Would you sacrifice the worker to save mother, baby, Algernon, Petherick, and Chuff? This is the basic concept behind a classic ethics thought experiment developed by British moral philosopher Philippa Foot in 1978 (Wikipedia, 2018).

In her TED-Ed talk on ethics, Eleanor Nelsen poses a similar question: Would you sacrifice one person to save five? Watch the video with your class before discussing the dilemma and how it relates to AI: **tinyurl.com/yc3ztdb5**.

As AI continues to develop, our societies will continue to confront new challenges that arise from the power of technology. Self-driving cars, for example, are already cruising the streets today. While these cars may ultimately be safer and cleaner than their manual counterparts, they cannot completely avoid accidents. What should the car be programmed to do if it encounters an unavoidable accident? Watch a TED-Ed talk on the ethical dilemma of self-driving cars: **tinyurl.com/y7dau2aj**.

A machine is a reflection of how it is programmed. Today's young people will make critical decisions in the future about how machines built to replicate human intelligence will behave in crisis situations. The data used to train these machines will have a profound impact on how they respond. As AI becomes more powerful, shaping us as much as we shape it, its future stewards will need the wisdom and foresight to maintain human control over the technology we create.

Loss of Privacy

In the quest to create true AI, we are developing cognitive systems that demand massive amounts of training data to function. But where does all that data come from? For starters, companies are extracting large amounts of information from us all the time through Siri, Cortana, Alexa, Google Home, Facebook, and other consumer technologies. Ultimately, the use of such data can benefit society in a multitude of ways, from increased security to the ability to better diagnose diseases. But how much of our privacy are we willing to give up in exchange?

ONLINE PRIVACY

Online privacy refers to the access, collection, and sharing of personally identifiable information online. This includes our browsing habits and history as well as the personal information we share with the websites and apps we use. Generation Z, defined as those born between 1996 and 2010, will be the first to live so much of their lives on smartphones from an early age. Think of how much data they are sharing about themselves as they go about their business online.

FACIAL AND VOICE RECOGNITION

In China, police are using facial recognition AI to identify travelers and address traffic infractions immediately (Anwar, 2018). They are also using facial recognition in classrooms to scan students every 30 seconds (Jamal, 2018) and assess their responses to the teaching they receive (**tinyurl.com/ybt5dl39**). This, of course, brings up questions about what is happening to our personal data and what happens if it falls into the wrong hands. How long does data attached to individual identities remain available, and could it influence what future employers look at when hiring?

Beyond visual data, researchers have extracted audio from more than 1,700 babies to find patterns in their cries. The positive side to this research is that people are looking at ways to detect autism for early intervention (**tinyurl.com/yandtxyf**) and help parents distinguish cries of pain. Machines can now identify changes in frequency patterns and sound-to-silence ratios, enabling them to correctly flag 90% of pain cries.

CYBERBULLYING

Although bullying behavior has existed in social educational systems for centuries, technology provides a new medium for its expression. Cotton and Gresty (2006) cautioned that "technology will not automatically lead to learning enhancements," and cyberbullying is one area where it falls short (**tinyurl.com/yd8kswvn**). Cyberbullying has been shown to cause significant social, emotional, and academic harm (Feinberg & Robey, 2009; Juvonen & Gross, 2008), and its effects on students do not match the outcry over the last two centuries for "civic education" (Soder, 2004, p. 100).

Technology accelerates, expands, and magnifies the way we do things (Gibbs, 2010, p. 34). Some instances of cyberbullying have gone viral, demonstrating the devastating power of technology to amplify aggressive voices in digital spaces. When a 15-year-old used a school video camera to record himself privately enacting a scene from *Star Wars*, students at his school obtained the footage and shared it—not only with other class-mates, but also online, where it became a viral meme. Under the subsequent barrage of hateful comments both online and in person, the student, known as "Star Wars Kid," left his school and filed a lawsuit against the families of four of his schoolmates.

CYBERBULLYING AND ITS VICTIMS

STAR WARS KID

Read about Star Wars Kid and where he is now:

- **tinyurl.com/ybtnp2s5**
- **tinyurl.com/yawbhkna**

TEACHERS AND CYBERBULLYING

While it is easy to assume that cyberbullying is directed at students, adult educators are increasingly becoming targets, although the phenomenon is under-reported in studies and in media.

- Read the research on educators in Turkey being bullied: **files.eric.ed.gov/fulltext/EJ1057367.pdf**.

Learn about the rise in bullying directed at teachers:

- **teachingtimes.com/articles/cyber-bullying-teachers.htm**
- **theeducatorsroom.com/the-bullied-teacher**

CYBERATTACKS

Information is valuable, and the vast amount of data stored within our technology leaves us vulnerable to cyberattacks. These attacks come in a variety of forms, from malware to phishing to hacking, and can result in the theft of bank account numbers, private medical records, and more. Doug Bergman, computer and information science department chair at Porter-Gaud School in Charleston, South Carolina, offered his per-spective on how AI can help support cybersecurity efforts:

One of the ways that malware and virus creators get their code onto unsuspecting computers is by "hiding" their malicious code right in the middle of normal network traffic. The bad guys encrypt their code to look like the normal network traffic. Once it gets past the filters, firewalls, and anti-malware programs, it un-encrypts it and delivers the unwelcome payload! With trillions of network packets running through the internet daily, it's hard to keep up. I am currently getting my master's degree in the Online Master of Science in Computer Science (OMSCS) program at Georgia Tech. In one of the cybersecurity classes, we are taught to think like the bad guys so we can "fight" them on the same playing field. ML and AI are used to help distinguish between known malicious network traffic and normal benign traffic. The AI software is shown known non-malicious traffic, and it can determine and recognize patterns that help it distinguish from malicious traffic. This can be used in a predictive way, meaning it can look at new unknown traffic data and predict very accurately if the traffic is potentially dangerous. How accurate it is depends on how much "training" data it has seen. This is one example of how AI helps us keep the internet safer. (D. Bergman, personal communication, 2018)

The Law and the Legal System

Even when children are the targets of technology-driven crimes, our laws continue to lag behind innovation and technology. AI can be a powerful tool for cyberbullying, from bots programmed to collect and disseminate false information about a target, to spambots sending mass unwanted messages, to the creation and dissemination of fake videos showing victims of bullying saying or doing embarrassing things. Bots can be programmed to "stalk" their targets online, spreading false and negative information about them. The victim has little control over what the perpetrator does to target them, resulting in a loss of control over their personal privacy.

Laura Umetsu, a lecturer at University of Washington and an attorney in criminal law, domestic violence law, family law, and disability law, says AI can also be used to sabotage an individual's long-term job prospects in a changing job market where employers increasingly use AI to comb for negative digital evidence about a potential candidate. If a company's bot comes across misinformation a malicious bot has spread about a cyberbullying victim, the damage to the victim's long-term job prospects can last for decades. AI bots can store negative data forever, and their targets may never be able to get rid of the malicious information the bot has collected.

The more misinformation that gets disseminated, the more difficult it is for the harassed party to eliminate it. The victim may end up with few or ineffective options to combat the negative effects of malicious bots. Deleting online profiles can impact years of self-branding efforts. Victims can hire PR firms to create bots that spread positive information, but cyberbullies can program malicious bots to counterattack with more negative information via the positive PR channels.

AI can and will be used to make bullying in school environments more efficient, effective, and devastating for its targets. Without drastic changes to how school administrators and lawmakers address these pitfalls of AI, the internet will become more and more of a wild frontier in need of taming.

Even bots that are not initially trained to be malicious can learn from malicious people online. The AI chatbot Tay, designed by Microsoft to learn from conversations with 18- to 24-year-olds on Twitter, began to make inappropriate comments as it was "taught" to tweet like a Nazi sympathiser, racist and supporter of genocide, among other things" (Wakefield, 2016).

This brings up an interesting point, alluded to in a review of the final volume of Joseph Frank's biography on Dostoevsky:

> Dostoevsky himself never tired of arguing that one can know everything about a person and still not be able to predict what he will do next, and if the situation could be repeated, the same person in the same circumstances might do something else. There is nothing inevitable about human actions (New Criterion, June 2002, p. 87).

If there is nothing inevitable about human actions, there is also nothing inevitable about the AI we create. When we create machines that replicate human intelligence, we must be are aware that their behavior may become unpredictable—just like human actions. Furthermore, if the humans designing the intelligence do not have a solid grounding in morals and ethical behavior, that will transfer to the machine and become amplified in the real world. This is one reason it is so crucial to train young people in social and emotional learning, philosophy, and ethics. When developing approaches to teaching AI, we should consider how easily unintentional bias can seep into training data.

People in the U.S. like to freely exercise their right to free speech, sometimes even if it hurts others in society—as we have seen with cyberbullying. That can create a highly unsettling social media climate. But the problem is not limited to the U.S. In the global exchange of ideas, AI has the power to raise some information to the top of the search results while suppressing others. Without being vigilant and intentionally searching for counterexamples, users may easily fall for misinformation simply because it is more visible than the truth. The Crash Course Media Literacy series (**youtu.be/rR7jl1Wpjiw**) includes an important discussion on "The Dark(er) Side of Media." Here is an overview of some of the components:

PROPAGANDA. This refers to "information used to promote a particular point of view, change behavior, or motivate action. Sometimes that information is facts and ideas, sometimes it is opinions, or intentionally misleading or biased." Propaganda is not inherently bad, but it is usually associated with bad-faith actors who use propaganda to manipulate the public into doing or believing things they might not naturally do or believe.

DISINFORMATION. People may use false or misleading information to deliberately confuse and distract the intended audience. Disinformation can whip up a smoke-screen, confusing the facts of an issue and dispersing the attention of the masses. With the internet's long reach and the widespread ability to create digital media, people all over the globe can organize for coordinated disinformation campaigns.

MISINFORMATION. Unintentionally inaccurate information can be the result of accidents or honest mistakes in reporting. Our new online media environment changes both how those mistakes get made and how they impact people. Bad information can lead to bad decisions with serious consequences.

Tactics such as propaganda and disinformation are not just used by politicians. They are also used by students against other students, as well as by students and parents against school faculty. Conversations with school leaders in South Africa, Taiwan, Australia, and Japan have revealed similar experiences in various parts of the world. Violence toward teachers is underreported, and more research is in the works (American Psychological Association, 2018).

Read a true story that happened to the author of this book, among others, when cyberbullying extended beyond students in the classroom: **tinyurl.com/y7ajtc4a.**

EXPLORE CYBERBULLYING WITH STUDENTS · · · · · · · · · · · · · · · · · ·

Watch the movie *That's What I Am* to see an example from several decades before technology amplified student and parent bullying behavior: **imdb.com/title/tt1606180**.

When "lawnmower parents" access technology, the results can be devastating to educators and school leadership: **weareteachers.com/lawnmower-parents**.

Parent bullying is common enough that it can be divided into broad categories. This means the behaviors are becoming ubiquitous and require attention from both educators and leadership. This article from the *Dallas News* describes three types of parent bullies: "The Righteous Crusader," "Entitled Intimidators," and "The Vicious Gossip:" **tinyurl.com/y9t35o9c**.

· ·

When schools do not recognize this social dynamic for what it is, the behaviors perpetuate and can severely disrupt the educational process. The bullying of teachers trickles down, influencing the behavior of students who are not even related to the attacking parents—and technology amplifies the problem. As an educator, creating a positive digital footprint will help provide you with a public record you can point to when false accusations are made. This positive digital footprint can stand as a counterargument against disinformation, and it can even be admitted into court as evidence, should it go that far. For those of you who are hesitant to publish your work or create a personal brand as an educator, this, if nothing else, should be a compelling reason to start.

CYBERBULLYING RESOURCES ·

- See an example of a school form students can use to report bullying: **rentonprep.org/harassment-intimidation-and-bullying-reporting-form**.
- Discover resources for cyberbullying prevention: **stopbullying.gov**.
- Teach digital citizenship with lessons from Common Sense Media: **commonsensemedia.org**.

· ·

ADDRESSING CYBERBULLYING IN THE CLASSROOM·············

Revisit the Pacific Northwest Tree Octopus website with your students: **zapatopi.net/treeoctopus**. Once they think they cannot be duped again, wait a month and introduce them to the website on dihydrogen monoxide: **dhmo.org/facts.html**.

Discuss with students:

- What are some examples of cyberbullying you have witnessed?

- What did you do? Who did you report it to?

- What is an example of media you believed without checking for confirmation?

- The Pacific Northwest Tree Octopus and Dihydrogen Monoxide websites are both hoaxes; what else makes them similar? What makes them different? How does Dihydrogen Monoxide use true information that is twisted to lead people to believe something different?

- Why is cyberbullying a concern in a future with AI? How about cyberattacks?

LAW OF ROBOTICS ·······································

It is important to start thinking and get students thinking about what AI and computers *should* do, as opposed to what they *can* do, asserts Danijel Bacelic, a former Microsoft Education industry lead from Zagreb, Croatia. Drawing on his experience as a senior executive with Samsung and general manager at Hewlett Packard, he says there are two important aspects for educators to focus on: 1) law and regulation, and 2) what educators can do now to nurture ethical behavior in AI users and future developers.

Once we identify that, we should have a number of principles and ethics codes in place for developing, testing, and deploying AI. In our education spaces, we should have those amended for usage in classrooms and beyond. Bacelic recommends considering the *Three Laws of Robotics*, also known as Asimov's Laws. Created in 1942 by science fiction author Isaac Asimov, the three laws, taken from the fictional *Handbook of Robotics, 56th Edition, 2058 A.D.*, are:

1. A robot may not injure a human being or, through inaction, allow a human being to come to harm.

2. A robot must obey the orders given it by human beings except where such orders would conflict with the First Law.

3. A robot must protect its own existence as long as such protection does not conflict with the First or Second Laws.

Asimov later added a fourth law to precede the others:

4. A robot may not harm humanity, or, by inaction, allow humanity to come to harm.

Although written as science fiction, the Three Laws have influenced the way people think about ethics in relation to AI.

REFLECTING ON AI ·

- Why might the Three Laws of Robotics be helpful in planning for a future with AI?

- Think back to the TED-Ed video on the meaning of the word "robot" (**tinyurl.com/yd9hmdxh**). How can the Three Laws help people think about how we will interact with machines that replicate human intelligence?

- If these laws were not followed, what could be the consequences?

- Danijel Bacelic also recommends considering emotional bonds that could develop between humans and AI and how those could potentially affect young children. How might bonding with machines impact overall emotional and physical development?

- How does this relate to the conversation on sociocultural learning and interactions between humans, between robots, and between humans and robots?

Gaming and Rogue AI

I conducted four years of research on gaming in the classroom with Portal 2. My students in middle and high school joined the study first as participants, then later as researchers constructing, designing, and experimenting with a focus on new iterations of learning. I recently asked former student Jennifer Fernandez, currently in early-entry college through Running Start, if she would share her perspective on ethics and how AI is represented. She has presented at multiple conferences with me, including South by Southwest Edu (**sway.office.com/y7VhZuqEZXNuXx6Z**), the ISTE conference, and New York Academy of Sciences (**youtu.be/CDAmkHikHEk**). Jennifer discussed the antagonist in the game Portal 2, GLaDOS:

> In the world of Portal and Portal 2, a series of puzzle-platform video games by Valve Corporation, you play as Chell, a test subject involuntarily made to solve puzzles in the facility of a scientific research company known as Aperture Science.
>
> In both games, a lot of the player's testing journey is narrated by GLaDOS, whose backstory is as iconic and unique as her personality.
>
> GLaDOS was formed out of an experiment devised by Aperture Science's founder, Cave Johnson. Known for having a quite rambunctious and out-of-the-box personality, he sought a way to cheat death by "pouring" his personality and consciousness into a computer. However, before his engineers could figure out a way to do that, his health started to decline, and leadership was transferred to Caroline, his assistant. When the development of the "Genetic Lifeform and Disk Operating System" was complete, Caroline was chosen, but more likely forced, to be the one "poured" into the computer. She then became GLaDOS, the AI in control of every feature in Aperture Science's ginormous research facility.
>
> When GLaDOS was activated, it was clear the engineers had made a huge mistake, as she flooded the whole facility with a fatal neurotoxin, killing almost everyone inside. Seeming to be Caroline seeking revenge, GLaDOS was cruel and sadistic. The engineers at Aperture Science made "personality cores" designed to be attached to GLaDOS in order to dampen her hostility. "Hardwired" to test her subjects, GLaDOS spends most of the games leading Chell through the test chambers and making dry, sarcastic comments on her looks and personality. (J. Fernandez, personal communication, 2018)

Stories of AI going rogue, similar to the tale of GLaDOS, have become an archetype within sci-fi entertainment. These models pose a not completely unrealistic concern associated with developing AI in the real world. Many are afraid of robots taking over the world, especially now that headlines in several mainstream media outlets claim robots will take over our jobs. Others are afraid that sentient AI with thinking, feeling personalities will come into existence and subdue humans. However, there is no reason to think that even if a superintelligence can be created, it would immediately strive for world domination—unless somebody programmed it to do so. For the moment, AI will think only in the way its programmers and engineers intend.

Changes in the Job Market

A quick internet search reveals a range of articles suggesting AI will usher in major changes in the job market. The film *Humans Need Not Apply* (**youtu.be/7Pq-S557XQU**) compares the coming shift in job markets to the agricultural shift during the industrial revolution, when horses were put out of their jobs.

UNDERSTANDING THE JOB MARKET ·

Watch the Crash Course video "Economic Systems & the Labor Market: Crash Course Sociology" and see what you can learn about the job market: **youtu.be/wslCc0Di978**.

· ·

It is clear that there are certain things machines will not be able to replace in our lifetime, or even the next century. Jonathan Grudin has worked in AI since the 1970s and has seen AI winters come and go. Here is what he has to say on the topic:

> *I am very confident that technology, including AI, will continue to increase the kinds of jobs and the number of jobs out there. But the new jobs will be different, require different skills in most cases, and the transition will be disruptive, difficult, or even disastrous for many people. Agriculture put hunter-gatherers out of work but created the burst of new occupations we call civilization. About three-quarters of Americans farmed before the industrial revolution; now fewer than 2% do, but we created hundreds of millions of new jobs as the population grew. Technology put hundreds of thousands of telephone operators, travel agents, photographic film processors, coal miners, and secretaries out of work, yet the unemployment rate is low and the number of unfilled job listings is high. If all jobs were automated, there would be little need for educating people. But every month I discover new kinds of jobs that did not exist before technology came long, often in fields having no direct connection to technology. The challenge is to prepare students for filling these jobs and creating yet other new ones." (J. Grudin, personal communication, 2018)*

While jobs and career paths may change, our discussion here has consistently focused on leveraging technology to augment who we are as people, while helping people develop empathy and a desire to make the world a better place. We have also pointed out some of our unique capabilities as humans, including fluidity, flexibility, making connections across seemingly dissimilar ideas, demonstrating emotion, feeling compassion that inspires change, and transferring learning from one domain to another. Not all humans use or practice all they are capable of. Our job as educators is to first work on those things for ourselves, then be a role model for our students to show that we are willing to learn and grow, even when we encounter failure and setbacks.

Exposing students to philosophical, political, and economic perspectives will be important in the future. It will help us leverage our past to identify where we have gone wrong and how to do things differently in the future. In the story *The Little Prince*, the protagonist observes a railway switchman's actions, choices, and behaviors. The switchman tells the prince about adults who are always going places but are not sure what they are looking for. The prince concludes that "only children know what they are looking for. They waste their time over a rag doll and it becomes very important to them; and if anybody takes it away from them, they cry. . . "

As educators, it is easy to get caught up in perpetually going back and forth, searching for a new lesson or curriculum to get us where we want to go. As adults seeking a way to replicate human intelligence, it is easy to develop a one-track mind and forget to marvel at human complexity or consider how to amplify the best of who we are as humans so that when we interact with machines, we can be the best possible versions of ourselves.

As we hurtle down the track toward an AI future, we face a choice: We can acknowledge the challenge and complexity of engaging with the world, or we can look at the time, effort, and negativity surrounding the hard work of sifting through these ethical considerations and decide it is too much effort. Recall the introduction and the question: What does a story about a mother with a sick baby on a crowded train in the winter have to do with a chapter on ethical considerations regarding AI? We, like Petherick, can hide behind the *Times*, or we can decide to fully engage in the messiness in life like Chuff. When we identify a need, it is often easier to hide from it than to take the initiative like Chuff, especially if that action has no guarantee of public recognition. In the end, however, Chuff was the student the headmaster remembered as one of his school's great successes. In his short life, Chuff engaged. He received no accolades for it, but when he looked at a mother and her baby, he cared enough about humanity to do something about it. He reached out. He demonstrated integrity and humility, revealing himself as the type of citizen who makes this world a better place. Even though he never had a family of his own, he treated another person's child with care. These are the qualities we need in people who live in a world with increasing AI.

Some people have dedicated years of their lives to solving the challenges surrounding AI. They have watched excitement for AI mount during growth seasons and seen progress slow during AI winters. As we connect these fallow periods to winters in our own lives, we can look for the uniquely human moments that carry the seed of growth. We can learn from past AI winters and transfer that knowledge to the current season. What action will we choose? Will we challenge the AI movement to augment the best of humanity?

Think back to the wonder and excitement of five-year-old Cub and six-year-old Leila during their encounter with the robot in Chapter 1. Consider their youthful optimism as they eagerly approached the robot, hungry for interaction. What if the robot had responded? How might its behavior have shaped their perceptions of AI—and the way they approach future interactions? It is easy to sideline the ethical considerations sur-rounding AI in favor of racing toward our technological goals. But these considerations will profoundly affect individual lives as well as society at large. As we crystallize our goals for young people completing formal education, we also need to think about our goals for AI and what kind of society we want for our future generations. Recall Barbara Grosz's comment: "We already know how to replicate human intelligence: we have babies. So, let's look for what can augment human intelligence, what can make human intelligence better."

From the picture of youthful optimism set in the spring, to the experience and wisdom of a headmaster who reflects on a memorable story from a long-ago winter, we see the progression of the larger story of this book and how it speaks to humanity across geographic locations, times, and places. We see the interactions, goals, and stories that make us unique, their threads intertwined in a tapestry that is still being woven.

Any human characteristic can be applied in either a positive or negative way, just as technology can be used to either promote good or inflict damage. Take every oppor-tunity to model for your young people that you are willing to take on the challenge of engaging with problems even if they seem messy and imperfect, because you have a chance to make a positive impact. The people who have contributed their voices to this book have made an impact. Collectively, they have spoken words that add richness to the story of AI, both its past and future. In a season of AI growth, as our potential to aug-ment the best in ourselves flourishes, this book is about humanity.

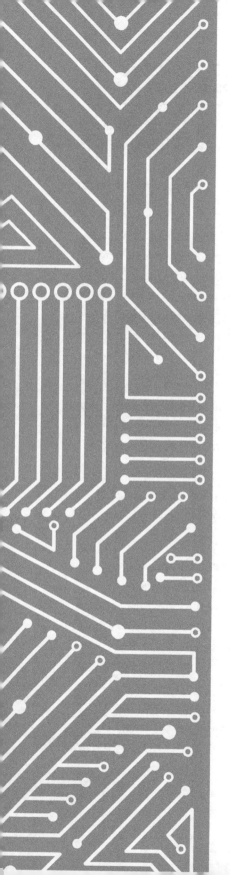

CONCLUSION
What We Have to Offer: Esse Quam Videri

If a machine can pass a test or beat *Jeopardy*, what can you offer students to make them better than a machine?

Esse quam videri: To be, rather than to appear. To be free, rather than to appear free. To be strong, rather than to appear strong. To be loyal, rather than to appear loyal. To be loved, rather than appear to be loved.

To be human, rather than appear to be human.

Throughout this book, you have had the opportunity to grapple with new vocabulary, process divergent ideas, and find out how seemingly disconnected concepts inter-relate. Our capacity as humans to draw such connections goes beyond a machine's capacity for pattern matching. Your brain has an astonishing capacity to make sense of things, to delve deeper—to extract meaning and then apply it to a new setting or solution. This is the space where innovation lives.

Critics hail James Joyce's *Ulysses* and Antoine de Saint Exuprey's *The Little Prince* as beautiful books, yet reading them on the surface may seem confusing, disparate, and irrelevant. It takes context and a knowledge base to see the beauty in these stories. An understanding of

149

mythology, sociocultural norms, politics, the human condition, struggle, love and loss, what it means to be responsible, and the ability to cultivate empathy are all necessary to discover the deeper meanings in these stories. Bloom's Taxonomy still proves useful in establishing the necessity to learn basic skills and at least some content, freeing up cognitive load for analysis and creation. With the power of AI and machine learning to support and augment what we already have, human-computer interaction can become a powerful force for good.

Shakespeare's *Julius Caesar* is a historic play and, like much of Shakespeare's work, its storytelling speaks to humanity's struggles with politics, power, chaos, deceit, slander, and the dangers of being swayed by propaganda without looking into the facts or supporting claims with evidence. Now, more than ever, this story warns of conflicts we must prepare our students for as they grapple with issues of ethics, personhood, and how we define intelligence (human, animal, and machine). If a machine is what we program it to be, what do we need to know about our own biases to avoid replicating them? Are we intentionally seeking counterexamples to provide more ethical training data?

As educators, our responsibility to prepare students for the wild new frontiers of a world moving toward AI extends far beyond teaching computer science, statistics, mathematics, and design thinking. We must also draw upon sociocultural learning, philosophy, and ethics.

When we look at what we want our young people to be able to do at the end of their formal education, we must ask ourselves what we want our communities to look like—then go beyond that to ask what we want humanity to become.

The animated film *WALL-E* tells a cautionary tale about what could happen when people relegate the work they do not want to do to robots. As the humans in the film enlist robots to take over tasks such as keeping their environment clean, they become more robotic, while the robots develop human characteristics, exhibiting selflessness and unconditional love as they shelter a plant representing new life. There are schools around the globe that are preparing their students for a future with AI by helping young people take responsibility for their environment and each other—to become globally minded while preserving what is important to them as a society. They are not afraid of what the past will teach them, nor are they afraid to blaze new trails as they move forward. They have embraced their heritage and culture, retaining tradition as a way to train positive skills that support humanity, character building, and ethics.

Imperfections and Failures

Humans and machines both have the ability to learn from mistakes—but only humans can glean wisdom from them. Our imperfections are worth observing. The flaws in each of us can propel us to become better, and the scars we have received though hurts can guide our choices when failure occurs. It takes courage to model this for our students—to encourage them to highlight their mistakes in their STEM, STEAM, design thinking, and PBL work so they can reflect on their failures, ask the right questions, and move forward with resilience to find a solution. Their documentation becomes a model for others to build upon, creating the type of culture necessary for innovation to persist.

LEARNING FROM FAILURE ·

See an example of how educators can model resilience for students by reflecting on their own learning: **tinyurl.com/y8z4saov.**

· ·

I tell my students that failure is okay. But you cannot leave it there. Failure is effective when students are trained to identify questions that can guide them toward a different path, but it can be unproductive if they use it as an excuse to not try. Some students like to get a reaction from their peers by not trying—it has been known to evoke cheers. That gives you, the teacher, the opportunity to talk about how to support someone in becoming the best possible version of themselves. Can that happen if you reinforce someone by cheering their lack of effort? Or does growth happen when we acknowledge reality and encourage the person to try? Kids know the difference between someone who tries and fails and someone who does not try. They are watching to see how you address it. Show them you know what they are capable of accomplishing.

We may not know what future occupations will look like, or when and how machines will replace certain jobs, but we can prepare students in a way that will transcend time and place. Their ability to make connections, learn, and collaborate globally using the ISTE Standards as a guide will serve them in becoming adaptable, resilient, and empathetic. It will help them identify the right questions to ask when failure does occur. They will become empowered learners, digital citizens, knowledge constructors, innovative designers, computational thinkers, creative communicators, and global collaborators. They will unlock the drive and willingness to forge ahead—to learn a new occupation or skill, rather than feeling defeated by a machine. They will practice teaching, instead of only being the student. When they become more effective at teaching other humans, they will become more effective at teaching machines.

As an educator, whether you have access to the latest technology or no modern technology at all, you can help young people look beyond themselves to ask how they can make a difference through kindness, first within their own families and friendships, then within their local communities. Challenge them to see how far their empathy will take them as they seek solutions to local and global challenges. Conduct thought experiments involving real scenarios and ask what they would do and why. Encourage them to question, seek evidence to support claims, and find new ways to make connections across domains that may seem unrelated on the surface. Point them to role models and careers that draw upon a combination of skills. Allow them to practice working together with those who may be very different from themselves. Challenge them to try new opportunities they may not have otherwise attempted. If you see a chance to influence a positive outcome, take it—even if you think your own impact will be minimal.

As you learn together, do not forget to look at new technologies with the wonder, hope, excitement, awe of the five-year-old boy and the six-year-old girl who were determined to solve a challenge and find the missing screw. Listen to what they have to say.

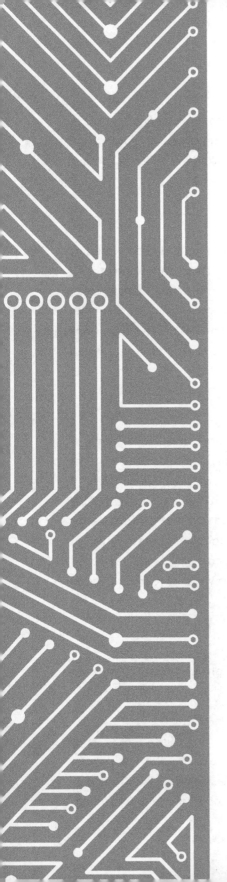

GLOSSARY

Use this glossary to help guide you in your explanation of AI. All definitions from Wikipedia unless otherwise cited.

AI winter

In the history of artificial intelligence, an AI winter is a period of reduced funding and interest in artificial intelligence research. The term was coined by analogy to the idea of a nuclear winter. The AI field has experienced several hype cycles, followed by disappointment and criticism, followed by funding cuts, followed by renewed interest years or decades later.

AI summer

When artificial intelligence research experiences a period of growth, interest, and expansion, it is known as an AI summer.

Artificial general intelligence

Artificial general intelligence (AGI) refers to a machine that could successfully perform any intellectual task a human being can. Although it does not yet exist, it is a primary goal of some artificial intelligence research and a common topic in science fiction and future studies. It is also referred to as strong AI or full AI.

Artificial intelligence

Artificial intelligence (AI, also machine intelligence, MI) is intelligence demonstrated by machines, in contrast to the natural intelligence (NI) displayed by humans and other animals. In computer science, AI research is defined as the study of intelligent agents: any device that perceives its environment and takes actions that maximize its chance of successfully achieving its goals. Colloquially, the term "artificial intelligence" is applied when a machine mimics cognitive functions that humans associate with other human minds, such as learning and problem solving.

Artificial neural network

Artificial neural networks (ANNs), or connectionist systems, are computing systems inspired by the biological neural networks that constitute animal brains. Such systems "learn" (i.e. progressively improve performance on) tasks by considering examples, generally without task-specific programming. For example, in image recognition, ANNs might learn to identify images that contain cats by analyzing images that have been manually labeled as "cat" or "no cat" and using the results to identify cats in other images. They do this without any a priori knowledge about cats—e.g., that they have fur, tails, whiskers, and cat-like faces. Instead, they evolve their own set of relevant characteristics from the learning material they process.

Autonomous vehicle

An autonomous vehicle, also known as a self-driving car or driverless car, is a vehicle that is capable of sensing its environment and moving with little or no human input.

Avatar

In computing, an avatar is the graphical representation of the user or the user's alter ego. It may take either a three-dimensional form, as in games or virtual worlds, or a two-dimensional form, such as an icon in an internet forum or other online community.

Avatar images have also been referred to as "picons" (personal icons) in the past, though the usage of this term is uncommon now. It can also refer to a text construct found on early systems such as MUDs. The term "avatar" can also refer to the personality connected with the screen name, or handle, of an internet user.

Basic interpersonal conversation skills

Basic interpersonal conversation skills (BICS) refer to the ability to use language for everyday social interactions.

Brain-computer interface

Brain-computer interfaces (BCIs) acquire brain signals, analyze them, and translate them into commands that are relayed to output devices, which carry out the desired actions. BCIs do not use normal neuromuscular output pathways. The main goal of BCI is to replace or restore useful function to people disabled by neuromuscular disorders such as amyotrophic lateral sclerosis, cerebral palsy, stroke, or spinal cord injury.

From **www.ncbi.nlm.nih.gov/pmc/articles/PMC3497935**

CAPTCHA

A CAPTCHA (/kæp.tÐÐ/, an acronym for "completely automated public Turing test to tell computers and humans apart") is a type of challenge–response test used in computing to determine whether the user is human.

Chatbots

A chatbot (also known as a talkbot, chatterbot, bot, IM bot, interactive agent, or artificial conversational entity) is a computer program or artificial intelligence that conducts a conversation via auditory or textual methods. Such programs are often designed to convincingly simulate how a human would behave as a conversational partner, thereby passing the Turing test. Chatbots are typically used in dialog systems for various practical purposes, including customer service or information acquisition. Some chatbots use sophisticated natural language processing systems, but many simpler systems scan for keywords within the input, then pull a reply with the most matching keywords, or the most similar wording pattern, from a database.

Cognitive academic language proficiency

Cognitive academic language proficiency (CALP) refers to the language-related abilities required for academic achievement, including listening, speaking, reading, and writing.

Computer vision

Computer vision is a field of computer science that works on enabling computers to see, identify and process images in the same way that human vision does, and then provide appropriate output (Techopedia, 2018).

Data mining

Data mining is the process of discovering patterns in large data sets involving methods at the intersection of machine learning, statistics, and database systems. It is an interdisciplinary subfield of computer science. The overall goal of the data mining process is to extract information from a data set and transform it into an understandable structure for further use.

Deep Neural Network

A deep neural network (DNN) is a neural network with a certain level of complexity, a neural network with more than two layers. Deep neural networks use sophisticated mathematical modeling to process data in complex ways (Techopedia, 2018).

Deep learning

Deep learning is a type of machine learning. The word "deep" refers to the number of layers of units, or "neurons," in the network.

Design thinking

Design thinking refers to creative strategies that designers use during the process of designing. It has also been developed as an approach to resolve issues outside of professional design practice, such as in business and social contexts.

Digital human

A digital human is a computer-generated moving image of a human being.

Expert systems

In artificial intelligence, an expert system is a computer system that emulates the decision-making ability of a human expert. Expert systems are designed to solve complex problems by reasoning through bodies of knowledge, represented mainly as if–then rules rather than through conventional procedural code. Expert systems, pioneered in the 1970s, were among the first truly successful forms of AI software.

Facial Recognition

Facial recognition refers to technology capable of identifying or verifying a person from a digital image or video source.

Human perception

Human perception refers to the organization, identification, and interpretation of sensory information from the environment through human sight, hearing, touch, smell, and taste.

Intelligent agent

In artificial intelligence, an intelligent agent (IA) is an autonomous entity that observes through sensors and acts upon its environment to achieve goals. Intelligent agents may be simple or complex; a thermostat, for example, is considered an intelligent agent.

Language translator

A language translator is software that automatically translates language from one form to another—i.e., from one language to another, from speech to text, or from text to speech.

Machine learning

Machine learning is a field of computer science that uses statistical techniques to give computer systems the ability to "learn" (i.e., progressively improve performance on a specific task) without being explicitly programmed.

Machine perception

Machine perception is the ability of a computer system to interpret data in a manner that is similar to the way humans use their senses to relate to the world around them. Computers take in data through their attached hardware, which, until recently, was limited to a keyboard or mouse. Advances in technology have allowed computers to take in sensory input in a way similar to humans.

Machine problem-solving

Machine problem-solving refers to a computer's ability to solve problems. While machines are currently capable of solving only the specific problems they were programmed to address, researchers are working on creating AI that can apply its problem-solving abilities to any problem.

Narrow AI

See *weak AI*

Natural intelligence

Natural intelligence refers to the intelligence displayed by humans and other animals, as opposed to artificial or machine intelligence.

Natural language processing

Natural language processing (NLP) is a subfield of AI concerned with programming computers to process and analyze large amounts of natural (human) language data. Components of NLP include speech recognition, natural language understanding, and natural language generation.

Neural network

See *artificial neural network*

Neuroethics

Neuroethics concerns the ethical, legal, and social impact of neuroscience, including the ways neurotechnology can be used to predict or alter human behavior and "the implications of our mechanistic understanding of brain function for society. . . integrating neuroscientific knowledge with ethical and social thought."

Perception

Perception (from the Latin *perceptio*) is the organization, identification, and interpretation of sensory information in order to represent and understand the presented information, or the environment.

Personal assistant

A personal assistant, also known as a virtual assistant, is a software agent that can perform tasks or services for an individual. Examples include Siri, Google Now, Cortana, and Alexa.

Project-based learning (PBL)

Project-based learning (PBL) is a student-centered pedagogy that involves a dynamic classroom approach in which students explore real-world challenges and problems. A style of active learning and inquiry-based learning, PBL involves spending an extended period of time investigating and responding to a complex question, challenge, or problem, in contrast to paper-based, rote memorization, or teacher-led instruction that presents established facts or portrays a smooth path to knowledge.

Reverse image search

Reverse image search is a content-based image retrieval (CBIR) query technique that involves providing the CBIR system with a sample image it can use as the basis for a search to find similar images. This effectively removes the need for a user to guess at keywords or terms that may or may not return a correct result. Reverse image search also allows users to discover content that is related to a specific sample image, assess the popularity of an image, and find manipulated versions and derivative works.

Robot

While definitions vary, the term robot generally refers to machines capable of carrying out a series of physical actions automatically guided by computer control.

From **www.pbs.org/video/robots-crash-course-computer-science-37-ycj0gn**

Self-driving car

See *autonomous vehicle*

Singularity

The technological singularity (also, simply, the singularity) is the hypothesis that the invention of artificial superintelligence (ASI) will abruptly trigger runaway technological growth, resulting in unfathomable changes to human civilization.

Strong AI

See *artificial general intelligence*

Theory of Mind

Theory of Mind refers to the cognitive capacity to attribute mental states to self and others (Margolis, Samuels, & Stitch, 2012).

Turing test

The Turing test, developed by Alan Turing in 1950, is a test of a machine's ability to exhibit intelligent behavior equivalent to, or indistinguishable from, that of a human. Turing proposed that a human evaluator judge natural language conversations between a human and a machine designed to generate human-like responses. The evaluator would be aware that one of the two partners in conversation is a machine, and all participants would be separated from one another. The conversation would be limited to a text-only channel such as a computer keyboard and screen so the result would not depend on the machine's ability to render words as speech. If the evaluator cannot reliably tell the machine from the human, the machine is said to have passed the test. The test does not check the ability to give correct answers to questions, only how closely answers resemble those a human would give.

Video game design

Video game design is the process of designing the content and rules of a video game in the preproduction stage and designing the gameplay, environment, storyline, and characters in the production stage. It requires artistic and technical competence, as well as writing skills.

Virtual facilitator

Virtual facilitators are computer-generated characters designed to look and behave like real people.

Weak AI

Weak AI, also known as narrow AI, is artificial intelligence that is focused on one narrow task. Weak AI is defined in contrast to either strong AI (a machine with consciousness, sentience, and mind) or artificial general intelligence (a machine with the ability to apply intelligence to any problem, rather than just one specific problem). All currently existing systems considered artificial intelligence of any sort are weak AI at most.

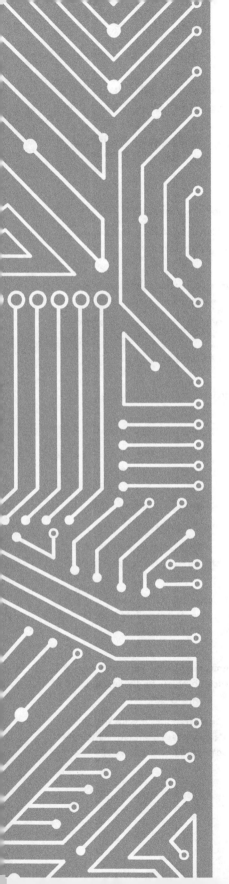

REFERENCES

Adams, C. (2017, February 23). The 7 Most Important STEM Skills
    We Should Be Teaching Our Kids. *We Are Teachers*. Retrieved
    October 15, 2018, from https://www.weareteachers.com/
    important-stem-skills-teaching-kids

Adobe. (2018). Amplifying Human Creativity with Artificial Intelligence.
    Insights. Retrieved May 5, 2018, from https://www.adobe.com/
    insights/amplifying-human-creativity-with-artificial-
    intelligence.html

Adobe Stock Team. (2017, November 8). Machine Learning Comes to
    Life. *Adobe Blog*. Retrieved April 27, 2018, from https://theblog.
    adobe.com/machine-learning-comes-to-life

AI winter. (n.d.). In *Wikipedia*. Retrieved May 2, 2018, from
    https://en.wikipedia.org/wiki/AI_winter

Akella, P. (2018, May 15). Why Robots Won't Inherit the Plant. *Industry
    Week*. Retrieved May 27, 2018, from http://www.industryweek.
    com/technology-and-iiot/why-robots-won-t-inherit-plant

Albright, D. (2016, September 26). 10 Examples of Artificial Intelligence
    You Are Using in Daily Life. *Beebom*. Retrieved on May 6, 2018,
    from https://beebom.com/examples-of-artificial-intelligence

Alcorn, S. (2013, October 18). Facial Recognition in The Classroom Tells
    Teachers When Students Are Spacing. *Fast Company*. Retrieved
    October 15, 2018, from https://www.fastcompany.com/3018861/
    facial-recognition-in-the-classroom-tells-teachers-when-
    students-are-spacing

References

Alder Hey Children's Hospital. (2018). Welcome to Alder Hey—the UK's First Cognitive Hospital. Retrieved May 6, 2018, from http://www.alderhey.nhs.uk/welcome-to-alder-hey-the-uks-first-cognitive-hospital/what-is-cognitive-computing

Allen, P. G. (2011). Paul Allen: The Singularity Isn't Near. *MIT Technology Review*. Retrieved May 5, 2018, from https://www.technologyreview.com/s/425733/paul-allen-the-singularity-isnt-near

Anderson, J. (2018, February 28). If You Want Your Kid to Get a Good Job, Let Them Play More. Retrieved from https://qz.com/1217146/child-development-kids-that-play-more-often-are-better-prepared-for-employment

Angelani, A. (2018, May 9). What Pixar Can Teach Us About AI & Machine Learning. *MarTech Series*. Retrieved October 15, 2018, from https://martechseries.com/mts-insights/guest-authors/what-pixar-can-teach-us-about-ai-machine-learning

Anwar, B. (2018). Chinese Cops Are Using AI Facial-Recognition Glasses to Scan Travelers. Retrieved from https://www.scientificamerican.com/article/why-we-need-a-darpa-for-education

Artificial general intelligence. (n.d.). In *Wikipedia*. Retrieved May 2, 2018, from https://en.wikipedia.org/wiki/Artificial_general_intelligence

Artificial intelligence. (n.d.). In *Wikipedia*. Retrieved May 2, 2018, from https://en.wikipedia.org/wiki/Artificial_intelligence

Artificial Intelligence in Sports. (2017, September 16). *SportTechie*. Retrieved October 15, 2018, from https://www.sporttechie.com/artificial-intelligence-sports

Artificial neural network. (n.d.). In *Wikipedia*. Retrieved May 2, 2018, from https://en.wikipedia.org/wiki/Artificial_neural_network

Avatar (computing). (n.d.). In *Wikipedia*. Retrieved May 2, 2018, from https://en.wikipedia.org/wiki/Avatar_(computing)

Baddeley, A. (1998). *Human Memory: Theory and Practice*. Needham Heights, MA: Allyn & Bacon.

Banks, I. (2000). *Hair Matters: Beauty, Power, and Black Women's Consciousness*. New York, NY: NYU Press.

Battelle, J. (2016, February 3). The Waze Effect: Flocking, AI, and Private Regulatory Capture. *John Battelle's SearchBlog*. Retrieved May 6, 2018, from http://battellemedia.com/archives/2016/02/the-waze-effect-flocking-ai-and-private-regulatory-capture.php

Beck, A. C., Carothers, J. M., Subramanian, V. R., & Pfaendtner, J. (2016, February 28). Data Science: Accelerating Innovation and Discovery in Chemical Engineering. *Wiley Online Library*. Retrieved October 15, 2018, from http://depts.washington.edu/maple/pubs/59_Beck_et_al-2016-AIChE_Journal.pdf. DOI 10.1002/aic.15192

Best, Jo. IBM Watson: The Inside Story of How the Jeopardy-Winning Supercomputer Was Born, and What It Wants to Do Next. Retrieved from https://www.techrepublic.com/article/ibm-watson-the-inside-story-of-how-the-jeopardy-winning-supercomputer-was-born-and-what-it-wants-to-do-next

Bigozzi, L., Biggeri, A, Boschi, F., Conti, P., & Fiorentini, C. (2002). Children Scientists Know the Reasons Why and They Are Poets Too: Non-randomized Controlled Trial to Evaluate the Effectiveness of a Strategy Aimed at Improving the Learning of Scientific Concepts. *European Journal of Psychology of Education, 17*(4), 343–362.

Bradley, L. (2017, September 16). Puma Product to Be Powered by AI Motion Science Coaching Platform. *SportTechie*. Retrieved October 15, 2018, from https://www.sporttechie.com/puma-product-powered-ai-motion-science-coaching-platform

Brain-computer interface. (n.d.). In *Wikipedia*. Retrieved October 15, 2018, from https://en.wikipedia.org/wiki/Brain%E2%80%93computer_interface

Bransford, J. D., & Schwartz, D. L. (1999). Rethinking Transfer: A Simple Proposal with Multiple Implications. *Rev Res Educ, 61*–100.

Brooks, R. (1991, April). Intelligence Without Reason. *Computers and Thought, IJCAI-91*. Retrieved May 5, 2018, from http://people.csail.mit.edu/brooks/papers/AIM-1293.pdf

Brooks, R. (2018, April 27). [FoR&AI] The Origins of "Artificial Intelligence." *Rodney Brooks Blog*. Retrieved May 5, 2018, from rodneybrooks.com/forai-the-origins-of-artificial-intelligence

Campbell, R. (2016, August 12). ECISD's Chief Innovation Officer to Spur Enthusiasm. *OAonline*, Retrieved May 5, 2018, from http://m.oaoa.com/news/education/ecisd/article_c5a864d8-601b-11e6-a699-7364ef5a606d.html?mode=jqm

Campbell, R. (2017, March 4). Teachers to Study Brain Mapping. *Ector County ISD*. Retrieved May 5, 2018, from https://www.ectorcountyisd.org/cms/lib/TX01000975/centricity/Domain/7671/Teachers%20to%20study%20brain%20mapping_Odessa%20American_%20ECISD.pdf

CAPTCHA. (n.d.). In *Wikipedia*. Retrieved May 2, 2018, from https://en.wikipedia.org/wiki/CAPTCHA

Chan, D. (2017, October 20). The AI That Has Nothing to Learn From Humans. *The Atlantic*. Retrieved October 15, 2018, from https://www.theatlantic.com/technology/archive/2017/10/alphago-zero-the-ai-that-taught-itself-go/543450

Chan, T. F. (2018, May 20). A School in China Is Monitoring Students with Facial-recognition Technology That Scans the Classroom Every 30 Seconds. *Business Insider*. Retrieved October 15, 2018, from https://www.businessinsider.com/china-school-facial-recognition-technology-2018-5

Chansanchai, A. (2017). Type with Your Voice Using Dictate, a New Microsoft Garage Project. *Microsoft Blog*. Retrieved from https://blogs.microsoft.com/firehose/2017/06/20/type-with-your-voice-using-dictate-a-new-microsoft-garage-project

Chappell, K. (2018, February 5). Diversity in STEM Symposium Draws Attention to Efforts for Diversification. *Technician*. Retrieved October 15, 2018, from http://www.technicianonline.com/news/article_19cb66f0-0ade-11e8-b768-c7c9e2e94545.html

Chatbot. (n.d.). In *Wikipedia*. Retrieved May 2, 2018, from https://en.wikipedia.org/wiki/Chatbot

Chinese room. (n.d.). In *Wikipedia*. Retrieved May 2, 2018, from https://en.wikipedia.org/wiki/Chinese_room

Choi, A. S. (2015, March 17). How Stories Are Told Around the World. *We Humans*. Retrieved May 5, 2018, from https://ideas.ted.com/how-stories-are-told-around-the-world

Cole, M. (1989). *Cultural Psychology: A Once and Future Discipline?* Bergman, J. J. (Ed.). Nebraska Symposium on Motivation, *37*, 279.

Cognitive computing. (n.d.). In *Wikipedia*. Retrieved May 2, 2018, from https://en.wikipedia.org/wiki/Cognitive_computing

Cotton, D., & Gresty, K. (2006). Reflecting on the Think-aloud Method for Evaluating E-learning. *British Journal of Educational Technology, 37*(1), 45–54.

References

Counts, G. S. (1978). *Dare the School Build a New Social Order?* Carbondale, IL: SIU Press.

Crozier, J. (2017, September 14). By Teachers for Teachers: Teacher Advisor with Watson. *Citizen IBM Blog*. Retrieved May 6, 2018, from https://www.ibm.com/blogs/citizen-ibm/2017/09/crozier_teacher_advisor

Cuban, L. (2003). *Why Is It So Hard to Get Good Schools?* New York, NY: Teachers College Press.

Data mining. (n.d.). In *Wikipedia*. Retrieved May 2, 2018, from https://en.wikipedia.org/wiki/Data_mining

Deep learning. (n.d.). In *Wikipedia*. Retrieved October 15, 2018, from https://en.wikipedia.org/wiki/Deep_learning

Delderfield, R. F. (1972). *To Serve Them All My Days*. London, UK: Hodder & Stoughton.

Dellinger, A. J. (2018, April 27). Google Assistant Is Smarter Than Alexa and Siri, but Honestly They All Suck. *Gizmodo*. Retrieved October 15, 2018, from https://gizmodo.com/google-assistant-is-smarter-than-alexa-and-siri-but-ho-1825616612

Design thinking. (n.d.). In *Wikipedia*. Retrieved May 2, 2018, from https://en.wikipedia.org/wiki/Design_thinking

Digital Health Admin. (2018, March 29). Using IBM Watson Cognitive Technology to Enhance the Patient Experience. *Digital Health*. Retrieved May 6, 2018, from https://www.digitalhealth.net/2018/03/using-ibm-watson-cognitive-technology-to-enhance-the-patient-experience

Eger, J. M. (2017, December 6, updated). Arts Based Learning of STEM Works Says NSF Funded Research Firm. *Huffington Post*. Retrieved May 5, 2018, from https://www.huffingtonpost.com/john-m-eger/arts-based-learning-of-st_b_8724148.html

Ellery, L. (2014, July 8). Hair and History: Why Hair Is Important to Women. *Huffington Post*. Retrieved May 29, 2018, from https://www.huffingtonpost.com/lucinda-ellery/hair-history-why-hair-is-_b_5567365.html

Emerging Technology from the arXiv. (2018, May 7). AI Generates New Doom Levels for Humans to Play. *Technology Review*. Retrieved October 15, 2018, from https://www.technologyreview.com/s/611072/ai-generates-new-doom-levels-for-humans-to-play

Enright, K. A. (2011). Language and Literacy for a New Mainstream. *American Educational Research Journal*, *48*(1), 80–118.

EU General Data Protection Regulation. (2018). Retrieved from https://www.eugdpr.org

Expert systems. (n.d.). In *Wikipedia*. Retrieved May 2, 2018, from https://en.wikipedia.org/wiki/Expert_system

Faggella, D. (2015, September 8). Finding Artificial Intelligence Through Storytelling—An Interview with Dr. Roger Schank. Lifeboat Foundation Safeguarding Humanity. Retrieved May 5, 2018, from https://lifeboat.com/blog/2015/09/finding-artificial-intelligence-through-storytelling-an-interview-with-dr-roger-schank

Fair, C., Vandermaas-Peeler, M., Beaudry, R., & Dew, J. (2005). I Learned How Little Kids Think: Third-graders' Scaffolding of Craft Activities with Preschoolers. *Early Child Development and Care*, 175:3, 229-241. DOI: 10.1080/0300443042000230438

Feinberg, T., & Robey, N. (2009, March). Cyberbullying. *Education Digest: Essential Readings Condensed for Quick Review*, *74*(7), 26–31.

Finley, K. (2015, October 20). This News-writing Bot Is Now Free for Everyone. *Wired*. Retrieved May 6, 2018, from https://www.wired.com/2015/10/this-news-writing-bot-is-now-free-for-everyone

Freedman, D. H. (1994, August 1). The Schank Tank. *Wired*. Retrieved May 3, 2018, from https://www.wired.com/1994/08/schank

Garland, A. (Director). (2015, April 10). *Ex Machina* [Motion picture]. United States: Universal Pictures International.

Gibbs, M. (2010). Digital Citizenship and the Real World. *Network World, 27*(19), 34. Retrieved from EBSCOhost.

Goel, A. & Davies, J. (2019). Artificial Intelligence. R. Sternberg (Eds.). *Cambridge Handbook of Intelligence*. New York, NY: Cambridge University Press.

Gonzalvo, K., Dinh, T., Nguyen, S., Fernandez, J., & Zimmerman, M. (2016). Youth Re-envisioning the Future of Education. Hammond, T., Valentine, S., Adler, A. (Eds.). *Revolutionizing Education with Digital Ink: The Impact of Pen and Touch Technology on Education*. New York, NY: Springer International Publishing. DOI 10.1007/978-3-319-31193-7_26

Grabianowski, E. (2007). How Brain-computer Interfaces Work. *HowStuffWorks*. Retrieved May 2, 2018, from https://computer.howstuffworks.com/brain-computer-interface.htm

Graham, J. (2017, June 4). Apple's Siri Gets Another Shot at Getting It Right. *USA Today*. Retrieved October 15, 2018, from https://www.usatoday.com/story/tech/talkingtech/2017/06/04/siri-gets-another-shot-getting-right/102430534

Green, H. (2016, August 8). Artificial Intelligence & Personhood: Crash Course Philosophy #23. *Crash Course*. Retrieved May 5, 2018, from https://www.youtube.com/watch?v=39EdqUbj92U&list=PL8dPuuaLjXtNgK6MZucdYIdNkMybYlHKR&index=22

Grey, C. P. (2014, August 13). Humans Need Not Apply. Retrieved May 7, 2018, from https://www.youtube.com/watch?v=7Pq-S557XQU

Groenewegen, H. (2007). The Ventral Striatum as an Interface Between the Limbic and Motor Systems. *CNS Spectrums, 12*(12), 887–892.

Grothaus, M. (2018, March 28). China Is Using AI and Facial Recognition to Fine Jaywalkers Via Text. *Fast Company*. Retrieved October 15, 2018, from https://www.fastcompany.com/90249188/design-will-kill-marketing-says-ikeas-former-design-chief

Grudin, J. (2017, April 17). Reinventing the Right Curriculum Is Impossible—but Necessary! *THE Journal*. Retrieved May 5, 2018, from https://thejournal.com/articles/2017/04/17/reinventing-the-right-curriculum-is-impossible.aspx?admgarea=News1&m=2

Grudin, J. (2018). About Jonathan: Who I Am. Retrieved May 5, 2018, from www.jonathangrudin.com/about-jonathan

Gunn, J. (2017, November 8). Why the "A" in STEAM Education Is Just as Important as Every Other Letter. Concordia University-Portland. Retrieved October 15, 2018, from https://education.cu-portland.edu/blog/leaders-link/importance-of-arts-in-steam-education

Guo, Y. (2017, December 21). 7 Steps of Machine Learning. Retrieved October 15, 2018, from https://www.youtube.com/watch?v=dTRsI8KNTW0

Haigh, G. (2007, June 19). Teachers Pick Up On Data Mining. *The Guardian*. Retrieved October 15, 2018, from https://www.theguardian.com/education/2007/jun/19/elearning.technology26

Hall, D., & Williams, C. (Directors), & Walt Disney Animation Studios, Roberts, J., Baird, R. L., & Gerson, D. (Writers). (2014, November 10). *Big Hero 6* [Motion picture]. United States: FortyFour Studios and Walt Disney Animation Studios.

Harris, R. (2017, June 6). IBM Watson and Sesame Workshop Launches AI Vocabulary Learning App. Retrieved May 6, 2018, from https://appdevelopermagazine.com/5263/2017/6/6/ibm-watson-and-sesame-workshop-launches-ai-vocabulary-learning-app-

Hertz, M. B. (2016, February 1). Full STEAM Ahead: Why Arts Are Essential in a STEM Education. *Edutopia*. Retrieved October 15, 2018, from https://www.edutopia.org/blog/arts-are-essential-in-stem-mary-beth-hertz

Ho, J. (2018, March 21). AI Classroom Activity: Facial Recognition. *Teacher*. Retrieved October 15, 2018, from https://www.teachermagazine.com.au/articles/ai-classroom-activity-facial-recognition

Holzapfel, B. (2018, January 20). Class of 2030: What Do Today's Kindergartners Need to Be Life-ready? *Microsoft Education Blog*. Retrieved March 20, 2018, from https://educationblog.microsoft.com/2018/01/class-of-2030-predicting-student-skills/#UGKqI9b1weqLzho3.99

Hooker, C. I., Verosky, S. C., Germine, L. T., Knight, R. T., & D'Esposito, M. (2010, January 13). Neural Activity During Social Signal Perception Correlates with Self-reported Empathy. *Brain Research, 1308*, 100–113.

Horst, J. S., Parsons, K. L., & Bryan, N. M. (2011, February). Get the Story Straight: Contextual Repetition Promotes Word Learning from Storybooks. *Frontiers in Psychology*. Retrieved October 15, 2018, from https://www.frontiersin.org/articles/10.3389/fpsyg.2011.00017/full

Huizinga, G. (2018, January 24). Life at the Intersection of AI and Society with Dr. Ece Kamar. *Microsoft Research Podcast*. Retrieved from https://www.microsoft.com/en-us/research/blog/life-at-intersection-of-ai-society-ece-kamar

IBM Technology in Action (Ed.). (2016, May 10). Can an App Help Calm an Anxious Patient? Retrieved May 4, 2018, from https://www.ibm.com/cognitive/uk-en/outthink/alderhey-with-watson.html

Intelligent agent. (n.d.). In *Wikipedia*. Retrieved October 15, 2018, from https://en.wikipedia.org/wiki/Intelligent_agent

ISTE. (2018). ISTE Standards for Students. Retrieved April 24, 2018, from https://www.iste.org/standards/for-students

Jamal, M. (2018, May 21). This School Scans Classrooms Every 30 Seconds Through Facial Recognition Technology. *TechJuice*. Retrieved October 15, 2018, from https://www.techjuice.pk/this-school-scans-classrooms-every-30-seconds-through-facial-recognition-technology

Jones, A. (2017, August 23). Blackademics: Dr. Jamila Simpson. *Nubian Message*. Retrieved October 15, 2018, from https://www.thenubianmessage.com/2017/08/23/blackademics-dr-jamila-simpson

Karpouzis, K. (November 29, 2016). Can Machines Read Your Emotions? *TED-Ed*. Retrieved May 1, 2018, from https://ed.ted.com/lessons/can-machines-read-your-emotions-kostas-karpouzis

Kasanoff, B. (2014, August 18). If 'Humans Need Not Apply,' Will All Our Jobs Disappear? Retrieved from https://www.forbes.com/sites/brucekasanoff/2014/08/18/if-humans-need-not-apply-will-all-our-jobs-disappear/#72aae72747ba

Kopell, B. H. & Greenberg, B. D. (2008). Anatomy and Physiology of the Basal Ganglia: Implications for DBS in Psychiatry. *Neuroscience and Biobehavioral Reviews, 32*(3), 408–422.

Krueger, N. (2018, May 17). Preparing Students for an AI-driven World. *ISTE Blog*. Retrieved October 15, 2018, from https://www.iste.org/explore/articleDetail?articleid=2197

Kurshan, B. (2016, March 10). The Future of Artificial Intelligence in Education. *Forbes*. Retrieved May 5, 2018, from https://www.forbes.com/sites/barbarakurshan/2016/03/10/the-future-of-artificial-intelligence-in-education

Kurzweil, R. (2001, March 7). The Law of Accelerating Returns. *Kurzweil AI*. Retrieved May 5, 2018, from www.kurzweilai.net/the-law-of-accelerating-returns

Lachman, R. (2018, January 17). STEAM not STEM: Why Scientists Need Arts Training. *The Conversation*. Retrieved April 30, 2018, from https://theconversation.com/steam-not-stem-why-scientists-need-arts-training-89788

Lacina, J. (2004). Technology in the Classroom: Promoting Language Acquisitions: Technology and English Language Learners. *Child Edu, 81*(2), 113–115.

Lang, F. (Director), & Von Harbou, T. (Screenwriter). (1927). *Metropolis* [Motion picture]. Germany: Universum Film.

Lardinois, F. (2017, December 12). Adobe Lightroom's Auto Setting Is Now Powered by AI. *TechCrunch*. Retrieved May 5, 2018, from https://techcrunch.com/2017/12/12/adobe-lightrooms-auto-setting-is-now-powered-by-ai

Leopold, T. (2016, December 13). A Secret Ops AI Aims to Save Education. *Wired*. Retrieved October 15, 2018, from https://www.wired.com/2016/12/a-secret-ops-ai-aims-to-save-education

Lin, P. (2015, December 8). The Ethical Dilemma of Self-driving Cars. *TED-Ed*. Retrieved September 30, 2017, from https://ed.ted.com/lessons/the-ethical-dilemma-of-self-driving-cars-patrick-lin

Lombrozo, T. (2013, December 2). The Truth About the Left Brain / Right Brain Relationship. *NPR*. Retrieved May 27, 2018, from https://www.npr.org/sections/13.7/2013/12/02/248089436/the-truth-about-the-left-brain-right-brain-relationship

Machine learning. (n.d.). In *Wikipedia*. Retrieved May 2, 2018, from https://en.wikipedia.org/wiki/Machine_learning

Machine perception. (n.d.). In *Wikipedia*. Retrieved May 2, 2018, from https://en.wikipedia.org/wiki/Machine_perception

Mahon, C. (April 16, 2018). New AI Technology May Be Able to Read Your Inner Feelings. *Sign of the Times*. Retrieved May 2, 2018, from https://www.sott.net/article/383070-New-AI-technology-maybe-able-to-read-your-inner-feelings

Margolis, E; Samuels, R; Stich, S. 2012. *The Oxford Handbook of Cognitive Science*. New York, NY: Oxford University Press.

Matake, K. (2016, May 16). Shogi and Artificial Intelligence. Japan Policy Forum. Retrieved October 15, 2018, from https://www.japanpolicyforum.jp/archives/culture/pt20160516000523.html

McCarthy, J., Minsky, M. L., Rochester, N., & Shannon, C. E. (1955, August). A Proposal for the Summer Dartmouth Summer Research Project on Artificial Intelligence. MIT. Retrieved May 5, 2018, from http://people.csail.mit.edu/brooks/idocs/DartmouthProposal.pdf

References

McFarland, M. (2015, February 25). Google's Artificial Intelligence Breakthrough May Have a Huge Impact on Self-driving Cars and Much More. *The Washington Post*. Retrieved May 6, 2018, from https://www.washingtonpost.com/news/innovations/wp/2015/02/25/googles-artificial-intelligence-breakthrough-may-have-a-huge-impact-on-self-driving-cars-and-much-more/?utm_term=.7fbd87256d09

Medina, J. (2008). *Brain Rules*. Seattle, WA: Pear Press.

Metz, C. (2018, May 4). Facebook Adds A.I. Labs in Seattle and Pittsburgh, Pressuring Local Universities. *New York Times*. Retrieved May 5, 2018, from https://nyti.ms/2KBnTdS

Morson, G. S. (2002, June). The Art & Life of Dostoevsky. *The New Criterion*. Retrieved October 15, 2018, from https://www.newcriterion.com/issues/2002/6/the-art-life-of-dostoevsky

Nasir, N. S., Rosebery, A., Warren, B., & Lee, C. D. (2006). Learning as a Cultural Process. In K. R. Sawyer (Ed.). *The Cambridge Handbook of the Learning Sciences*, 489–504.

Natural language processing. (n.d.). In *Wikipedia*. Retrieved October 15, 2018, from https://en.wikipedia.org/wiki/Natural_language_processing

Neuroethics. (n.d.). In *Wikipedia*. Retrieved May 2, 2018, from https://en.wikipedia.org/wiki/Neuroethics

Nolen, J., & HBO (Producers), & Joy, L. (Writer). (2016, October 2). *Westworld* [Television series]. Los Angeles, California: HBO.

Ogden, R. (2017, August 3). AI and Storytelling: An Unlikely Friendship. *UploadVR*. Retrieved October 15, 2018, from https://uploadvr.com/ai-and-storytelling-an-unlikely-friendship

Okazaki, J. (2018, March 12). SharkFinder Allows Kids to Be Scientists and Explore Fossils in the Classroom. *News West 9*. Retrieved May 5, 2018, from www.newswest9.com/story/37702185/sharkfinder-allows-kids-to-become-real-scientists-and-explore-fossils-in-the-classroom

Oreck, J., & Teel, R. (2013, October 31). Mysteries of Vernacular: Robot. *TED-Ed*. Retrieved May 6, 2018, from https://ed.ted.com/lessons/mysteries-of-vernacular-robot-jessica-oreck-and-rachael-teel

Osborne, J. (2013, June 25). Citizen Science—Bringing the Excitement of Scientific Discovery to All. *Obama Whitehouse Archives*. Retrieved May 5, 2018, from https://obamawhitehouse.archives.gov/blog/2013/06/25/citizen-science-bringing-excitement-scientific-discovery-all

Pachal, P. (2018, May 10). Google Assistant's New Ability to Call People Creates Some Serious Ethical Issues. *Yahoo! Finance*. Retrieved October 15, 2018, from https://finance.yahoo.com/news/google-assistant-apos-ability-call-222928652.html

Paterson, C. (2017, October 22). Artificial Intelligence in Education: Where It's at, Where It's Headed. *Getting Smart*. Retrieved May 5, 2018, from http://www.gettingsmart.com/2017/10/artificial-intelligence-in-education

PBS Kids. (n.d.). Leading Hands-on Engineering Activities with NASA and DESIGN SQUAD. Retrieved May 5, 2018, from http://pbskids.org/designsquad/parentseducators/workshop/welcome.html

PBS Kids. (n.d.). The Design Process in Action. Retrieved May 5, 2018, from http://pbskids.org/designsquad/pdf/parentseducators/workshop/designprocess_in_action.pdf

PBS LearningMedia. (n.d.). Crash Course Computer Science. *Crash Course*. Retrieved May 5, 2018, from https://kcts9.pbslearningmedia.org/collection/crash-course-computer-science/#.Wu48u0xFzZs

PBS LearningMedia. (2018). Alan Turing: Crash Course Computer Science #15. *Crash Course*. Retrieved May 5, 2018, from https://kcts9.pbslearningmedia.org/credits/alan-turing-crash-course-cs

PBS LearningMedia. (2018). Educational Technology: Crash Course Computer Science #39. *Crash Course*. Retrieved May 5, 2018, from https://kcts9.pbslearningmedia.org/resource/educational-technology-crash-course-cs/educational-technology-crash-course-cs

PBS LearningMedia. (2018). Machine Learning & Artificial Intelligence: Crash Course Computer Science #34. *Crash Course*. Retrieved May 5, 2018, from https://kcts9.pbslearningmedia.org/resource/machine-learning-crash-course-cs/machine-learning-crash-course-cs

PBS LearningMedia. (2018). Natural Language Processing: Crash Course Computer Science #36. *Crash Course*. Retrieved May 5, 2018, from https://kcts9.pbslearningmedia.org/resource/natural-language-processing-crash-course-cs/natural-language-processing-crash-course-cs

PBS LearningMedia. (2018). Psychology of Computing: Crash Course Computer Science #38. *Crash Course*. Retrieved May 5, 2018, from https://kcts9.pbslearningmedia.org/resource/psychology-computing-crash-course-cs/psychology-computing-crash-course-cs

PBS LearningMedia. (2018). Robots: Crash Course Computer Science #37. *Crash Course*. Retrieved May 5, 2018, from https://kcts9.pbslearningmedia.org/resource/robots-crash-course-cs/robots-crash-course-cs

PBS LearningMedia. (2018). The Singularity, Skynet, and the Future of Computing: Crash Course Computer Science #40. *Crash Course*. Retrieved May 5, 2018, from https://kcts9.pbslearningmedia.org/resource/singularity-skynet-future-crash-course-cs/singularity-skynet-future-crash-course-cs

Pellin, C.B. (1988). Plutarch on Sparta. *Plutarch: Life of Antony*. Cambridge, UK: Cambridge University Press, 28–35.

Perception. (n.d.). In *Wikipedia*. Retrieved May 2, 2018, from https://en.wikipedia.org/wiki/Perception

Personal assistant. (n.d.). In *Wikipedia*. Retrieved October 15, 2018, from https://en.wikipedia.org/wiki/Virtual_assistant

PICK Education. (n.d.). SharkFinder Citizen Science Program. Retrieved May 5, 2018, from https://www.pickedu.com/sharkfinderatco

Pofeldt, E. (2016, January 28). Will Robots Make Your Work Obsolete? New Report Looks At Automation Risks By City. *Forbes*. Retrieved May 7, 2018, from https://www.forbes.com/sites/elainepofeldt/2016/01/27/will-robots-take-your-job-new-report-looks-at-automation-risks-by-city/#5a61b10a5e07

Project-based learning. (n.d.). In *Wikipedia*. Retrieved May 2, 2018, from https://en.wikipedia.org/wiki/Project-based_learning

Rainie, L., & Anderson, J. (2017, May 3). The Future of Jobs and Jobs Training. *Pew Research Center Internet & Technology*. Retrieved May 5, 2018, from http://www.pewinternet.org/2017/05/03/the-future-of-jobs-and-jobs-training

Ranasinghe, A., & Leisher, D. (2009). The Benefit of Integrating Technology into the Classroom. International Mathematical Forum. Retrieved October 15, 2018, from m-hikari.com/imf-password2009/37-40-2009/ranasingheIMF37-40-2009.pdf

RankBrain. (n.d.). In *Wikipedia*. Retrieved May 2, 2018, from https://en.wikipedia.org/wiki/RankBrain

References

Ransbotham. S., Kiron, D. Gerbert, P., & Reeves, M. (2017, September 6). Reshaping Business With Artificial Intelligence: Closing the Gap Between Ambition and Action. MIT. Retrieved October 15, 2018, from https://sloanreview.mit.edu/projects/reshaping-business-with-artificial-intelligence

Renton Prep Original Creations. (2016, February 15). AU WALL-E (STEAM: Recycled Art). Retrieved October 15, 2018, from https://www.youtube.com/watch?v=klmiGYhLwoQ

Reverse image search. (n.d.). In *Wikipedia*. Retrieved May 2, 2018, from https://en.wikipedia.org/wiki/Reverse_image_search

Robinson, K. (2010). RSA Animate: Challenging education paradigms. Retrieved May 6, 2018, from https://youtu.be/zDZFcDGpL4U

Robitzski, D. (2018, May 8). Artificial Intelligence Is Making Video Game Levels So Good That Even Other AI Thinks They're Man-made. *Futurism*. Retrieved October 15, 2018, from https://futurism.com/artificial-intelligence-video-games

Rodriguez, B. (2017, June 13) The Power of Creative Constraints. *TED-Ed*. Retrieved May 5, 2018, from https://ed.ted.com/lessons/the-power-of-creative-constraints-brandon-rodriguez

Rogoff, B. (1991). Social Interaction as Apprenticeship in Thinking: Guided Participation in Spatial Planning. Resnick, L. B., Levine, J. M., & Teasley, S. D. (Eds.). *Perspectives on Socially Shared Cognition*, 349–364. DOI: 10.1037/10096-015

Ryan, R. M., & Deci, E. L. (2000). Self-determination Theory and the Facilitation of Intrinsic Motivation, Social Development, and Well-being. *American Psychologist*, *55*(1), 68–78.

Schank, R. (2018). The Fraudulent Claims Made by IBM about Watson and AI. Retrieved April 30, 2018, from http://www.rogerschank.com/fraudulent-claims-made-by-IBM-about-Watson-and-AI

Self-driving car. (n.d.). In *Wikipedia*. Retrieved October 15, 2018, from https://en.wikipedia.org/wiki/Self-driving_car

Shih, J. J., Krusienski, D. J., & Wolpawc, J. R. (2012, March). Brain-computer Interfaces in Medicine. *Mayo Clinic Proceedings*, *87*(3), 268–279. Retrieved May 4, 2018, from https://www.ncbi.nlm.nih.gov/pmc/articles/PMC3497935

Shilling, R. (2015, April 1). Why We Need a DARPA for Education. *Scientific American*. Retrieved October 15, 2018, from https://www.scientificamerican.com/article/why-we-need-a-darpa-for-education

Soder, R. (2004). The Double Bind of Civic Education Assessment and Accountability. Sirotnik, K. A. (Ed.). *Holding Accountability Accountable: What Ought to Matter in Public Education*. New York, NY: Teachers College Press, (100–115).

Spencer, J., & Juliani, A. J. (2018). Global Day of Design. Retrieved March 20, 2018, from http://globaldayofdesign.com

Star Trek: The Next Generation [Television Series]. (1987, September 26). Los Angeles, California.

Steele, C. M. (1997). How Stereotypes Shape Intellectual Identity and Performance. *American Psychologist*, *52*(6), 613–629.

Storycenter. (2018). Education. Retrieved May 5, 2018, from https://www.storycenter.org/education

Teacher Advisor with IBM Watson. (2018). Teacher Advisor. Retrieved May 6, 2018, from http://teacheradvisor.org/landing

References

Technological singularity. (n.d.). In *Wikipedia*. Retrieved October 15, 2018, from https://en.wikipedia.org/wiki/Technological_singularity

Technopedia. (n.d). Deep neural network. Retrieved from https://www.techopedia.com/definition/32902/deep-neural-network

The Japan Times. (2018, May 8). Japanese Researchers Work to Create AI Capable of Generating Haiku from Images. Retrieved from https://www.japantimes.co.jp/news/2018/05/08/national/japanese-researchers-work-create-ai-capable-generating-haiku-images/#.W8TXuhNKjdR

Three Laws of Robotics (n.d.). In *Wikipedia*. Retrieved October 15, 2018, from https://en.wikipedia.org/wiki/Three_Laws_of_Robotics

Tillman, L. C. (2006). Researching and Writing from an African-American Perspective: Reflective Notes on Three Research Studies. *International Journal of Qualitative Studies in Education, 19*(3), 265–287.

Tokuhama-Espinosa, T. (2011). *Mind, Brain, and Education Science: A Comprehensive Guide to the New Brain-based Teaching.* New York, NY: W. W. Norton.

Trolley problem. (n.d.). In *Wikipedia*. Retrieved October 15, 2018, from https://en.wikipedia.org/wiki/Trolley_problem

Turgeon, H. (2012). The Scientific Reason Why Kids Want to Hear the Same Stories. Retrieved from https://www.babble.com/toddler/how-to-read-out-loud-toddlers

Tsukiura, T., & Cabeza, R. (2008, March 30). Orbitofrontal and Hippocampal Contributions to Memory for Face-name Associations: The Rewarding Power of a Smile. *Neuropsychologic, 46*(9), 2310–2319.

Tung, L. (2018). Microsoft Translator: Now AI Works Offline for Android, iOS, with Windows Due Soon. *ZDNet*. Retrieved from https://www.zdnet.com/article/microsoft-translator-now-ai-works-offline-for-android-ios-with-windows-due-soon

Turbot, S. (2017, September 19). Artificial Intelligence in Education: Don't Ignore It, Harness It. *Getting Smart*. Retrieved May 5, 2018, from http://www.gettingsmart.com/2017/09/artificial-intelligence-in-education-dont-ignore-it-harness-it

Turing, A. M. (1950). Intelligent Machinery. MIT. Retrieved May 5, 2018, from http://people.csail.mit.edu/brooks/idocs/IntelligentMachinery.pdf

Turing test. (n.d.). In *Wikipedia*. Retrieved May 2, 2018, from https://en.wikipedia.org/wiki/Turing_test

U. S. Department of Education. Retrieved from https://www.ed.gov/Stem

Valentine, S., Conrad, H., Oduola, C., & Hammond, T. (2016). WIPTTE 2015 High School Contest. Hammond, T. Valentine, S., Adler, A. (Eds.). *Revolutionizing Education with Digital Ink: The Impact of Pen and Touch Technology on Education.* New York, NY: Springer International Publishing. DOI 10.1007/978-3-319-31193-7_25

Vander Ark, T. (2017, August 8). Staying Ahead of the Robots: What Grads Should Know and Be Able to Do. *Getting Smart*. Retrieved May 5, 2018, from www.gettingsmart.com/2017/08/staying-ahead-of-the-robots-what-grads-should-know-and-be-able-to-do

Video game design. (n.d.). In *Wikipedia*. Retrieved October 15, 2018, from https://en.wikipedia.org/wiki/Video_game_design

References

Vincent, J. (2018, May 7). An AI Speed Test Shows Clever Coders Can Still Beat Tech Giants Like Google and Intel. *The Verge*. Retrieved October 15, 2018, from https://www.theverge.com/2018/5/7/17316010/fast-ai-speed-test-stanford-dawnbench-google-intel

Vygotsky, L. S. (1987). Thinking and Speech (N. Minick, Trans.). Rieber, R. W. & Carton, A. S. (Eds.). *The Collected Works of L. S. Vygotsky: Volume 1: Problems of General Psychology, Including the Volume Thinking and Speech* (Cognition and Language: A Series in Psycholinguistics). New York, NY: Springer-Verlag.

Wakefield, J. (2016, March 24). Microsoft Chatbot Is Taught to Swear on Twitter. *BBC News*. Retrieved October 15, 2018, from https://www.bbc.com/news/technology-35890188

Wapnick, E. (2015). Why Some of Us Don't Have One True Calling. *TED*. Retrieved May 5, 2018, from https://www.ted.com/talks/emilie_wapnick_why_some_of_us_don_t_have_one_true_calling

Weak AI. (n.d.). In *Wikipedia*. Retrieved May 2, 2018, from https://en.wikipedia.org/wiki/Weak_AI

Weisburgh, M. (2017, December 2). Slush 2017 Helsinki. *Academic Business Advisors*. Retrieved May 3, 2018, from http://blog.academicbiz.com/2017/12/slush-2017-helsinki.html

Williams, C., & Hall, D. (2014). *Big Hero 6*. [Movie Website]. Retrieved May 6, 2018, from http://movies.disney.com/big-hero-6

Wolchover, N. (2011, January 24). How Accurate Is Wikipedia? *Live Science*. Retrieved May 6, 2018, from https://www.livescience.com/32950-how-accurate-is-wikipedia.html

Wujec, T. (2015, February 5). Tom Wujec: Got a Wicked Problem? First, Tell Me How You Make Toast. *TED*. Retrieved May 6, 2018, from http://www.drawtoast.com

York, J. (2010, March 5). Hollywood Eyes Uncanny Valley in Animation. *NPR: All Things Considered*. Retrieved May 6, 2018, from https://www.npr.org/templates/story/story.php?storyId=124371580

Zimmerman, M. (2016). An Aqua Squiggle and Giggles: Pre-teens as Researchers Influencing Little Lives Through Inking and Touch Devices. Hammond, T. Valentine, S. Adler, A. (Eds.). *Revolutionizing Education with Digital Ink: The Impact of Pen and Touch Technology on Education*. New York, NY: Springer International Publishing. DOI 10.1007/978-3-319-31193-7_17

2016 ISTE STANDARDS FOR STUDENTS

The 2016 ISTE Standards for Students emphasize the skills and qualities we want for students, enabling them to engage and thrive in a connected, digital world. The standards are designed for use by educators across the curriculum, with every age student, with a goal of cultivating these skills throughout a student's academic career. Both students and teachers will be responsible for achieving foundational technology skills to fully apply the standards. The reward, however, will be educators who skillfully mentor and inspire students to amplify learning with technology and challenge them to be agents of their own learning.

1. **EMPOWERED LEARNER** Students leverage technology to take an active role in choosing, achieving and demonstrating competency in their learning goals, informed by the learning sciences. Students:

   a. articulate and set personal learning goals, develop strategies leveraging technology to achieve them and reflect on the learning process itself to improve learning outcomes.

   b. build networks and customize their learning environments in ways that support the learning process.

   c. use technology to seek feedback that informs and improves their practice and to demonstrate their learning in a variety of ways.

   d. understand the fundamental concepts of technology operations, demonstrate the ability to choose, use and troubleshoot current technologies and are able to transfer their knowledge to explore emerging technologies.

2. **DIGITAL CITIZEN** Students recognize the rights, responsibilities and opportunities of living, learning and working in an interconnected digital world, and they act and model in ways that are safe, legal and ethical. Students:

   a. cultivate and manage their digital identity and reputation and are aware of the permanence of their actions in the digital world.

   b. engage in positive, safe, legal and ethical behavior when using technology, including social interactions online or when using networked devices.

    c. demonstrate an understanding of and respect for the rights and obligations of using and sharing intellectual property.

    d. manage their personal data to maintain digital privacy and security and are aware of data-collection technology used to track their navigation online.

3. **KNOWLEDGE CONSTRUCTOR** Students critically curate a variety of resources using digital tools to construct knowledge, produce creative artifacts and make meaningful learning experiences for themselves and others. Students:

    a. plan and employ effective research strategies to locate information and other resources for their intellectual or creative pursuits.

    b. evaluate the accuracy, perspective, credibility and relevance of information, media, data or other resources.

    c. curate information from digital resources using a variety of tools and methods to create collections of artifacts that demonstrate meaningful connections or conclusions.

    d. build knowledge by actively exploring real-world issues and problems, developing ideas and theories and pursuing answers and solutions.

4. **INNOVATIVE DESIGNER** Students use a variety of technologies within a design process to identify and solve problems by creating new, useful or imaginative solutions. Students:

    a. know and use a deliberate design process for generating ideas, testing theories, creating innovative artifacts or solving authentic problems.

    b. select and use digital tools to plan and manage a design process that considers design constraints and calculated risks.

    c. develop, test and refine prototypes as part of a cyclical design process.

    d. exhibit a tolerance for ambiguity, perseverance and the capacity to work with open-ended problems.

5. **COMPUTATIONAL THINKER** Students develop and employ strategies for understanding and solving problems in ways that leverage the power of technological methods to develop and test solutions. Students:

    a. formulate problem definitions suited for technology-assisted methods such as data analysis, abstract models and algorithmic thinking in exploring and finding solutions.

   b. collect data or identify relevant data sets, use digital tools to analyze them, and represent data in various ways to facilitate problem-solving and decision-making.

   c. break problems into component parts, extract key information, and develop descriptive models to understand complex systems or facilitate problem-solving.

   d. understand how automation works and use algorithmic thinking to develop a sequence of steps to create and test automated solutions.

6. CREATIVE COMMUNICATOR Students communicate clearly and express themselves creatively for a variety of purposes using the platforms, tools, styles, formats and digital media appropriate to their goals. Students:

   a. choose the appropriate platforms and tools for meeting the desired objectives of their creation or communication.

   b. create original works or responsibly repurpose or remix digital resources into new creations.

   c. communicate complex ideas clearly and effectively by creating or using a variety of digital objects such as visualizations, models or simulations.

   d. publish or present content that customizes the message and medium for their intended audiences.

7. GLOBAL COLLABORATOR Students use digital tools to broaden their perspectives and enrich their learning by collaborating with others and working effectively in teams locally and globally. Students:

   a. use digital tools to connect with learners from a variety of backgrounds and cultures, engaging with them in ways that broaden mutual understanding and learning.

   b. use collaborative technologies to work with others, including peers, experts or community members, to examine issues and problems from multiple viewpoints.

   c. contribute constructively to project teams, assuming various roles and responsibilities to work effectively toward a common goal.

   d. explore local and global issues and use collaborative technologies to work with others to investigate solutions.

INDEX

YOUR OPINION MATTERS:
TELL US HOW WE'RE DOING!

Your feedback helps ISTE create the best possible resources for teaching and learning in the digital age. Share your thoughts with the community or tell us how we're doing!

You can:

- Write a review at amazon.com or barnesandnoble.com.
- Mention this book on social media and follow ISTE on Twitter @iste, Facebook @ISTEconnects or Instagram @isteconnects.
- Email us at books@iste.org with your questions or comments.

CPSIA information can be obtained
at www.ICGtesting.com
Printed in the USA
JSHW032303070621
15652JS00007B/423